NOURISH

Encouragement for Parents Homeschooling
Through High School

CARA MCLAUCHLAN

Cover by Courtney Sanford Design, www.courtneysanford.net

Nourish - *Encouragement for Parents*

Homeschooling Through High School

Copyright 2021 by Cara McLauchlan

Published by Vellum and IngramSpark

ISBN 978-1-7360439-0-5 (pbk.)

ISBN 978-1-7360439-1-2 (eBook)

The Library of Congress has cataloged the edition as follows:

McLauchlan, Cara

Nourish, encouragement for parents homeschooling through high school/Cara McLauchlan.

ISBN 978-1-7360439-0-5 (pbk.)

Names and identities have been changed for privacy.

For Russ, the catalyst in the great adventure.

Homeschooling is a worthy path. Whether you choose it purposefully or circumstances dictate it, there is beauty in it.

Some reading this may have homeschooled since birth and are looking for encouragement. Others have never home-schooled or even want to homeschool. Take heart. Whether you find yourself here happily or not, I promise there is good-ness in this season. I believe every parent has the ability to homeschool. It's about trusting yourself to do it. With God's help, you absolutely can.

Most of us would do anything for our kids. If your child was sick, you would traverse the Grand Canyon and back to get care for your child. With deep love, you would walk through burning coals for your kid. Homeschooling is about harnessing the same passion to pour into your child's heart and mind.

Many of us don't feel equipped to do this. Perhaps you don't feel you can handle hard classes. Remember, all of it isn't entirely up to you. You are designing a feast of ideas for your student, but you don't have to cook every course. There never will be a teacher more dedicated to managing their education than you. You are the exact right person to do this.

I wrote this companion to offer encouragement for the journey through the high school years. With love, dedication, prayer, and effort, this season will equip your family beyond measure. You've done it for years, whether you have homeschooled formally or not. You've taught them how to walk, talk, appreciate manners, and honor values. You've nourished and nurtured them their entire life. You know their hearts. You are dedicated to bringing out God's best in them. No one will ever take this task as seriously as you will. This alone is what makes you the absolute best teacher for them.

Please know my opinions are only one idea. Also, I only homeschooled one child, which has blessings and difficulties all its own. Families homeschooling multiple children have their own unique set of blessings and difficulties. My journey may not look like yours, but we all have similar ambitions.

Most everyone sets off to homeschool based on love. Sometimes we come from places of brokenness, desperation, heartache, or longing. However we arrive here, we can all agree that homeschooling is our chance to let God direct our days to foster greatness in our kids. This is no easy task, but it is a lovely one and worthy of our time.

This book is to remind you to stay fierce for this calling. The world needs your family to be an example of doing hard things for God. He will equip you if you trust Him; there is no greater work than to pour out love for your family. Homeschooling is a way to encourage our families to see God at the heart of it all. It is a worthy path.

Stay Fierce in Him,
    Cara McLauchlan
    2021

```
┌─────────────────────────────────┐
│                1                │
│                                 │
│            Starting             │
│          CHAPTER ONE            │
└─────────────────────────────────┘
```

Ideas and equipping to begin your homeschool journey.

"Do not despise small beginnings, for the Lord rejoices to see the work begin." Zechariah 4:10 (NLT)

"Look to the Lord and his strength; seek his face always."
Psalm 105:4

Homeschooling isn't for the faint of heart. Do yourself a favor and if you decide to homeschool this season, be all in. Starting out wishy-washy makes for a tough time for everyone.

As you begin, first make sure homeschooling is for you and your child. Maybe you don't have a choice, maybe you do. Talk to God. Look for His nudges and direction. If you think it is the path God is leading you down, know with certainty that you and your child are on the same path. I have met plenty of parents who decided for their students without any input. It is painfully obvious their kids hate every minute of every day. They battle with their parents constantly. Invite your child into the decision by praying and discussing it thoroughly as a family.

We all have doubts in everything. We all want an absolute guarantee with homeschooling to deliver a Harvard-bound, full-ride scholar, grounded in faith and motivated to save the world. However, the results can never be known for sure. There are no guarantees that homeschooling means perfection or success. As with any form of education -- public, private, charter or homeschool -- there is no absolute certainty your child will thrive and succeed.

Certainly, do all the things you know beforehand to have confidence in your decision. Do your research. Know what all your school options are, evaluate your resources and talents, pray about it, and look to God for direction and confirmation.

The high school years are particularly hard for doubters like me. It feels like a high stakes game when you think your child's future success in life depends on you. Yet is that really true?

Is it true high school was the complete and ultimate thing shaping your success in life? Maybe. Most likely not. High school absolutely gives you tools in your toolbox. I look back on my high school years and the most memorable equipping I received was from a typing class and working for a fast-food restaurant.

Yes, high school is important and we want to give our kids as many resources as possible. However, this season is not the only one giving them what they need to launch into the world. This is simply the season your family is in and there will be many more equipping seasons to come.

As you begin, decide you will do this for one year. When it's over, then evaluate. Or if you are like my friend Anne, decide you are staying on this path until God taps you on the shoulder and tells you otherwise. Think about the kind of year that makes your child's soul come alive. Gather input from your child for emotional investment in their education, too. This is your child's practice for taking ownership of their future.

Most importantly as you begin, be all in for the year. The greatest torture is the parents who second guess every move they make and constantly want you to know how much they are struggling. They are the obvious ones because their kids see their doubts and begin to reflect those, making everyone miserable.

Remember, nothing pursued out of love is ever lost. As you commit to the beginning of a school year, decide this will be a year of love no matter what. Even when it is hard, drama-filled, accomplished, or beautiful, this time spent with loved ones will be yours to keep. All of the golden memories -- good, bad, or otherwise -- will never be lost. Be all in.

Think
Ask God to direct your path for the year. What is He whispering in your heart about His plans for your family?

The Homeschooling Secret

"And now these three remain: faith, hope and love. But the greatest of these is love.". 1 Corinthians 13:13

I began homeschooling after my son finished third grade. On the last day of school, he was like a little old man. He wasn't sleeping. He was anxious and stressed all the time. It was no way to live for a nine-year-old.

Veteran homeschoolers told me sometimes kids need a year to heal from life in a traditional school setting. With that idea as my inspiration, I kept things simple. We read armloads of good books. We took field trips every week. We cooked and baked and painted. We used a simple math curriculum. We visited every museum in our town on a regular basis. Homeschooling was like a beautiful season flowing over my family all year long.

Watching my son bloom that year was like someone handing me gold every day. Certainly, there were days I cried and days he cried. There were days I didn't think I could handle math or the daily grind of it all. However, the Lord was faithful to see us through that sweet first year. We all learned so much and grew closer as a family. Witnessing the growth, love, and confidence in my son spurred us on to continue.

Now many years later, here I am homeschooling high school. With fear and trembling I ask myself, "Why do I homeschool again?" Suddenly things become serious when I'm counting on this education to get my son into college or pursue whatever his future plans hold. I pray the equipping will allow my child to pursue his dreams. When I began the high school years, my days started with the question, "Will it be good enough?"

Later as the high school years continued, God began to shift my prayers from, "Is it good enough?" to "God can You make it enough?" I asked God to fill in where I fell short. I prayed God would show our family no matter how inadequate we are, Jesus is more than adequate. I asked God to show my child how to be a passionate and engaging learner. Even though my efforts would never be enough, I trusted we serve a God who is enough in everything.

Whether you homeschooled since birth or you are beginning homeschooling, I believe there is something special about families making this commitment. Regardless of the education style and curriculums, we are all bound together out of a vast love. Because homeschooling is a process of the heart, it can't help but change everyone in the process.

I am grateful we chose this path. It entrenched me deep into a life example of walking by faith and trusting in Him. I will never regret a single day of homeschooling. It has blessed me beyond my wildest imaginations. It has taught me so much about myself. The honor and privilege to homeschool alongside some amazing parents enriched my life beyond measure. Having a front row seat for my son's moments of discovery and learning has been a blessing beyond compare.

The secret about homeschooling is that it's not about education. Homeschooling is about love. It's lavishing and nurturing your family in such a way that you are showing them the love of the Creator. It's exploring the world with the idea that everything points to Him. It's demonstrating to our kids that having faith and walking in it is the very best thing. The fruit of homeschooling is an equipping in how to be strong, courageous, curious, Christian young men and women. If we can get the most important thing right, loving God first, then all the other things will fall into place.

The secret about homeschooling is it's not about school at all. It's about love.

Think
How can you make your homeschooling about loving God first?

What's Your Why?

"...Always be prepared to give an answer to everyone who asks you to give the reason for the hope that you have. But do this with gentleness and respect..." 1 Peter 3:15

Everyone comes to homeschooling from a different place. Regardless, it is absolutely essential to be clear on your "why." Make your homeschooling why worthy of the task. Most importantly, be ready to share it with others.

How you speak about your why will dictate your heart and attitude. Make your why for homeschooling something that inspires. Saying homeschooling was your destination of last resort won't cut it. Let your daily words fuel your mindset.

At the start of a school year with gorgeous fall days, it was easy to know my "why." New schedules, classes, and experiences are vibrant and interesting during the beginning weeks of school. My why came easily in those fresh days. It was not so easy to know my why in January when I was sick with a cold and facing eye rolls from a moody teenager.

Your why isn't only for your equipping, it's also about the ordinary conversations. These casual chats can be your undoing if you aren't careful. Well-meaning people can sneak

11

attack you about homeschooling when you least expect it. I remember being all dressed up and happy about getting out of the house with my husband for a company dinner. Everything was going along in a lovely way until the casual discussion with my husband's colleague turned into an all-out debate over homeschooling.

I found myself fumbling over my words as I tried to recall all my smart data points about homeschooling to sound intelligent. All the diligence I dedicated to finding quality classes, excellent plans and experiences was forgotten in the moment. In the end, I convinced no one and ended up doubting and criticizing myself for not having a better answer. I didn't have my "why" ready. I was ambushed by others who were speaking out of assumptions and biases not founded in truth. I didn't tell my story well, even though I had a good story to tell.

If our hope comes from Christ, then all we do is an extension of that, including homeschooling. We need to be prepared to share the hope we have, with gentleness and respect.

In the early days of homeschooling, when people asked me why, I launched into a monologue of facts, figures, success rates, and statistics, immediately generating instant eye-glazing and face-melting boredom.

Later, when people asked me why, I began asking what they wanted to know. People always responded with the big thing they had already made up their mind about. Typically, this meant concerns about my child having friends or how I could teach hard subjects like physics. Ultimately, what they wanted to know is how a homeschooler could ever get into a college, especially a good one.

I found the more I let people talk about their thoughts on homeschooling, the easier it was to share my why with gentleness and respect. When I let them explain homeschooling to me, they sounded increasingly ridiculous, even to themselves. Ask a lot of questions from people who question you. Listen thoroughly first. Deeply listen longer than you want. Keep listening some more. Then share with gentleness and respect.

Remember, not everyone is going to think you are building up the kingdom through homeschooling. Some people will never get it. Forget about them. Your critical relatives may never understand your choice, even though they can plainly see what a fantastic child you have. Love those critical relatives anyway.

One of the most important things you can do to support confidence in homeschooling is to be ready with your why. It looks and feels much like defending your faith because that's where it starts. It is knowing why you are walking this path with Christ. It is giving an answer for the hope you have with gentleness and respect. You have a beautiful story to tell. Be prepared to tell it well.

Think
What is your why? How can you tell it well?

My Big Fat Homeschool

"...And I pray that you, being rooted and established in love, may have power, together with all the Lord's holy people, to grasp how wide and long and high and deep is the love of Christ, and to know this love that surpasses knowledge--that you may be filled to the measure of all the fullness of God." Ephesian 3:17-19

Start your homeschool season with a big fat vision for your year. Give yourself and your student permission to imagine something grand. Ask your family, "What would the school of our dreams look like?"

When I first considered homeschooling, my husband and I were on a road trip as we brainstormed our ideal school. We dreamed boldly about our child's education including hands-on learning, excellent books, real world experiences, travel, sports, foreign language tied to family history, time with grandparents, outdoor time, learning that was an ecosystem, not a box or a building. We longed for the freedom to design and customize our child's education in a passionate way.

If you are going to do this with joy, why not dream big? Create a big fat vision of what you and your student would love. Don't get caught up in a traditional school framework. Yes, you need to meet the state's criteria in order to graduate. Certainly, find out what the government requires for coursework. More importantly, don't let those requirements own you.

Design your child's education with the unique character, personality, learning style, dreams, and loves your student has in their heart. Decide what legacy your child's education might be and make that your grand vision. Don't be afraid to do things differently or to go against the grain of modern culture. Together, decide your family. vision and start creating a feast of ideas to nourish your student.

For our family, we wanted a potluck of learning. Truly, we thought about it like a fantastic buffet. Over the years, we had some traditional classes, on-line classes, hybrid classes, community college classes, short lab intensives, volunteer experiences, music, community co-ops, a couple of AP classes, as well as some test prep mixed in over longer periods of time. My child was passionate about science courses and history. Starting with this idea, we tailored his education to go deep in the areas where he especially loved.

As part of your brainstorming journey, be sure to include your child in planning the year. Share with them the requirements to graduate so they understand you aren't dictating their entire schedule. Creating ownership and investment in the high school journey is key. If your student feels as though you are deciding everything for them and they have no input, they will resent you and ultimately sabotage your good intentions. Include them in the process and empower them to plan a schedule aligning with some of their hopes and dreams.

The beauty of homeschooling is found when you and your student design a vibrant mix of experiences and classes matched to your family. Don't be afraid to create your own school style which reflects your personal family vision. We homeschool in order to take God-sized dreams and pair them to the hearts and minds of our children. We homeschool to bring out the best in our children with Him in mind.

Think
What is your family's God-sized vision for your homeschool?

Think Biggish

*"In the beginning you laid the foundations of the earth,
and the heavens are the work of your hands." Psalm 102:25*

We serve a big God. I'm regularly in awe of this idea, yet I
sometimes forget and want to do things small. Taking risks
and doing hard things feels like too much work. However, if
we serve a big God, He has called us to live boldly. In my
desire for comfort, I want to do things the same way I've done
them before. Yet God didn't invite me to homeschool to do it
small and safe.

If this is your first year of homeschooling, simply starting
to homeschool is plenty thinking big enough. However, if you
have homeschooled in the past, consider dedicating this year
to God in a deeper way. If you dared to do things a shade
better, where would it take you? How has God called you to
design your year? Where can you take a risk for God out of
love?

For me, it's tempting to do things which look good in the
eyes of culture. It's easy for me to be swayed by what our
friends are doing. Yet to fully embrace the beauty of home-

schooling, I need to ask: "Does this serve my family?" "Does this serve God?" and "Is this God's best for our year?"

This year, I feel like God is calling me to think big, or maybe only biggish. "Biggish" sounds doable to me. Whenever I hear the expression, "think big!" I feel as though I have to launch a company, run a triathlon or fast for ninety days. Yet when I hear "biggish," it doesn't sound as hard.

This year our family decided to let our student volunteer one day a week at a non-profit. We felt it was important for him to have real-world experiences through working with an organization he cared about. We wanted him to know what it was like to work in an office setting, be accountable to a boss and how to manage his time.

We also made plans for a once-in-a lifetime summer trip to Italy. My son had been studying Latin for four years and loved the history of the Latin culture. We planned and saved up for a year. In our hearts, we felt it was important to go deeper than only reading and studying the history of ancient times. We wanted him to know it from seeing and touching those places in person. We longed for an opportunity for history to come alive for him.

Lastly, my son wanted to dedicate his efforts to a higher level of ice hockey. This required a commitment of training, time, and physical demand my son had never experienced before. He wanted to challenge himself and as a family, we dedicated our time and resources. It required juggling of his schedule and studying on the road, but my son wanted to see what it was like to play ice hockey at the next level.

Everyone's "big" is different. Perhaps travel, sports, or volunteering aren't significant for you. For our family, we hoped to create meaningful experiences with our school year beyond what we studied in books and what we did during the week.

Your path will look different from everyone else's. In fact, this is what makes it your path. I'm grateful we serve a personal God. I'm grateful He gives us the freedom to explore, dream, and go deeper in our own ways of learning. Make your path worthy of the calling you have received in Him.

Think
How can you think biggish with your homeschool year?

Tools of the Trade

"Lord, you alone are my portion and my cup; you make my lot secure." Psalm 16:5

When I dreamed up our ideal homeschool space, I imagined it to look like the stylish Pinterest-perfect images on social media.

The heartwarming spaces fascinated me with their cute, matching baskets, stylish furniture and organized supplies in sweetly labelled cubbies. I imagined cozy reading nooks, spacious desks with every supply imaginable and bookshelves lined with every great book we could possibly need or want. I loved seeing how veteran homeschoolers created their school spaces for smart organization, creativity and efficiency.

The more I studied different homeschool workspaces, the more I realized it was truly personal for each family. Because we serve a personal God, it makes sense we can extend that personal love to our school spaces. Just as there is no one right way to homeschool, there is no one right way to set up your school space.

I found the more casual homeschool families liked to work

in a variety of spaces, with a basket of resources they could lug from place to place. Others worked entirely at the kitchen table in order for the parent to work nearby. Still others had a formal classroom set up, with real desks, real shelving, chalkboards, bulletin boards and organized resources all organized to access when needed.

Simple, complex, charming or spartan, your classroom only needs to be what works for your family. Here are a couple thoughts you might consider for setting up your classroom workspace.

What's your child's style? Does your child get distracted easily? Would they like a more structured environment? Or would they thrive best when they are in the midst of things and can ask questions as needed if you are nearby? What sort of environment would suit them best to focus, be productive and healthy?

For me personally, I chose an area away from the kitchen in order to create some literal and physical space from the school environment. Depending on your living area, this may or may not be possible for you. I wanted it to be separate, but not closed off like a bedroom. This way I could check in on my child, but not have to be on top of him while he did school. You will need to decide what works best for your family.

What resources are essential? I think it's especially important to have a designated work area. This does not necessarily mean a desk. It does need to be a place where they can spread out their books, resources, tools, and papers. This might mean a kitchen table, a lap desk in your family area or a quiet corner of your home. Also having all the school supplies and resources accessible is important. This might include paper, pencils, dry erase markers and dry erase boards, reference books, notecards.

Every student is an individual and you will need to tailor it to your student's style. Invite them to brainstorm what they need at the beginning of the year to set them up for success. It's also a nice practice for your student to make their school supply list, look up prices and set a budget for their resources. Then have them shop for the supplies and challenge them to stick as close as they can to their budget.

As you progress further in your homeschool season, you might consider helpful extras to support you. This may include books, on-line websites, or other study/education resources to consider as you go. For our family, having quality literature on hand and readily accessible was helpful. I liked having great books always available for road trips, time spent in the car, downtime or family vacations. Sometimes we read them together or other times, my student enjoyed them on his own. But having your favorites ready to go helps keep the big picture goals of your homeschool in mind during the over-whelm of the day to day.

Lastly, think of your homeschool environment as a constant work in progress. You may need to tweak things and change things as you go. If your child is struggling, they may need to work side-by-side with you during difficult seasons. Other times, they may enjoy the freedom and independence of managing their own day-to-day without you. The important thing is to check in on regular basis to see what things are working and what areas could use some polishing.

Remember, just as we are always being molded and shaped by God, so too will our homeschools be molded and shaped to bring out our child's best. Be open to constantly improving and adjusting your tools and your environment to nurture your child during the school year.

In every season, your homeschool will evolve to suit you as your needs change. Make it a constant work in progress to make it work for you and your family.

<u>Think</u>

What is your ideal homeschool setup? What resources and tools do you need to bring out the best in your family?

```
┌─────────────────────────────────────┐
│                                       │
│                                       │
│           Heartsongs                  │
│                                       │
└─────────────────────────────────────┘
```

"We don't choose what we will do for God; He invites us to join Him where He wants to involve us." Henry T. Blackaby, *Experiencing God*

Author Eric Davis describes his passion for becoming a Navy Seal as, *"having the song in you."*

In his book, *Raising Men*[1], Davis said wanting to be a Seal was something which never left him. At times, during the hard days of his training it burned low, almost like a pilot light on a stove, barely detectable. But the desire never left him and was always ready like a fire to be stoked. He said it was a constant song in his heart.

In many ways, I believe the education journey is about discovering your student's "song" as a family. One of the gifts of the homeschooling path is to design an environment which allows your student to find their song. Whether it's through books, academics, mentors, field trips, clubs or hobbies, home-schoolers can create learning ecosystems however they desire and in whatever way suits them best.

For me, my heartsong is writing. It is the thing that makes me feel like me. I believe I become more of the person God intended when I spend time writing. Even as a kid, the song was there. I would spend hours creating little books out of paper. From around the age of ten, I filled and saved dozens of scrapbooks, journals, and written adventures. Writing was always my heartsong. Yet I didn't know it.

Even though now it is truly obvious, I don't think I knew it until well into my thirties. As parents who homeschool, we can take the time to point out our children's gifts. What a blessing for our students to begin their launch in life knowing how God has gifted them. On a daily basis, we can shine light into their lives and reflect back what we see in them.

Truly, not every homeschooling student knows with clarity how God calls them. The beauty of homeschooling is we have time to explore this love with our kids. Keep in mind, if your homeschool is so busy with activity, you may need to carve out space to discover more of your student's dreams.

Ultimately, helping your student find their heartsong is about discovering what is already there. It's seeing with new eyes what is at work and what your student is already passionate about.

If you are looking to help your student find their heart-song, try being a bit of a detective. It might be ridiculously obvious, or you might have to dig a bit deeper. Invite them to consider what things they lose themselves in, what they are intensely curious about, what passions and hobbies fuel their days. These questions make easy conversations during car rides across town or waiting for your table at a restaurant. It can be as simple as looking at what they love, right now, together.

Discovering your student's heartsong doesn't have to be found through box-checking-style assessments or evaluated according to the world's standards. As parents, we get to serve as lights to point them in the direction of how God may be calling them. Make your homeschooling days sing to the tune of your child's heartsong. You will never regret the time spent with the people you love, helping them find what they love.

Think
How can you encourage your student to find their heartsong? What "songs" do you already see at work in your child?

[2] *Henry T. Blackaby, Experiencing God*

Start as You Mean to Continue

"Show me, Lord, my life's end and the number of my days; let me know how fleeting my life is." Psalm 39:4

When I first started homeschooling, I loved rules.

I was ridiculously over-the-top about keeping meticulous records of attendance, health, academics, grades, service, and extracurricular activities. It was almost as if I thought someone from the government was going to knock on my door at any moment. I wanted to do it right and be ready if I was ever called into question.

At first, I thought this was a good practice. Later I realized this system was not sustainable. If I was going to like myself and homeschooling, I had to release some things. As I progressed, I learned there were only a limited number of things which truly mattered.

Attendance and health records were important, but I only had to think about them once a year. The same was true for tracking every grade, every activity, every scrap of information about my homeschool. At some point, I simplified it all to only what was essential. Ongoing lists were all I needed.

As you begin your homeschool year, think about what

systems you need to put into place to keep track of things. Start as you mean to continue. In other words, don't make it so cumbersome and clunky that it becomes a heavy burden. Find ways to keep it simple and not allow your systems to get in your way.

Find a framework that works for you. This might be a fancy spreadsheet or writing things down on a calendar. Figure out your style and play around with it. You will probably tweak things as you go. Your end goal is to consider systems that become effortless for your family.

For me, I tried to "chunk" the administration part of homeschooling into seasons. During the summer, I researched and figured out what things I would like to include in our year. I included my child in the process by inviting him to share what he would like his year to look like. I set up some simple documents listing each of the classes, course descriptions, books, and details about what the course would cover.

For ongoing work, I had a huge metal box on my student's desk where completed or graded work was kept for filing. Twice a year, I would go through it and see if there was anything I wanted to save. Into an annual binder went anything I wanted to capture for the year. This might include essays, projects, photos, tests, awards, or anything with sentimental value.

At the end of the year, I added more things to the binder, filled in grades, standardized test scores, and any special awards, or notes I wanted to remember for the future. For high school, I kept a simple document as an ongoing transcript based on how I thought my son was doing and also based on his final scores at the end of the year.

These are a few ideas for what systems worked for my family. My encouragement is for you to discover systems that work for you. Don't get bogged down in the details of tracking your homeschool. Find out what is required by your state for reporting. Absolutely be a good steward for the homeschooling community in the way you track and report. Yet, don't let those systems own you or be your undoing. Above all keep it simple without overthinking things.

Decide your personal style for your homeschool and put systems in place to support you well. Make it easy to keep track of things. If you are not organized, invite your student to help you or make it part of their day to do it with you. Find ways to document your homeschool well. After all, it's your family story and no one will be able to tell it as well as you can. Make your story a good one with systems to track the many adventures you have each school year.

Think
What systems can you put in place to track your homeschool story?

Make It Yours

"You became imitators of us and of the Lord, for you welcomed the message in the midst of severe suffering with the joy given by the Holy Spirit." 1 Thessalonians 1:6

How do you make your homeschool a reflection of your family?

In our homeschool, we started with loves. Sometimes this may not be easy to do with algebra, physics, or British literature. With a little creativity, it is possible. Imagine it's the end of your student's high school years, what do you want them to carry forward in their toolkit for life? What is your family passionate about and how can you weave that into your homeschool days?

When I first started homeschooling, I wanted it to appear like a "real" school. I made every effort to replicate the traditional school experience with the exact same textbooks, curriculum, and class structure. This didn't last long when we both realized it was about as inspiring as shoveling coal.

School doesn't need to look like sitting at a desk for eight hours a day. Learning can be in a classroom, on-line, with a mentor, working, outside, reading books, or volunteering. It can be field trips, doing homework at a coffee shop, reviewing with friends, or reading at the library. It can be mowing the lawn for physical education, grocery shopping for the family, cooking dinner, or watching a history documentary over lunch. It can be getting together with a friend to conduct an experiment or build a rocket. Truly, it can be whatever you dream up.

Over the years, we longed for enriching experiences that looked nothing like a class. Music appreciation could be studying piano formally or attending concerts, plays, or productions. Spending time in nature with a journal allowed us to learn about our environment and practice observation skills with wildlife, birds, and rocks. Building rollercoasters, trebuchets, and PVC structures in our garage allowed us to tinker with physics, engineering, and design. Learning can be many things beyond a class, a book, or a lecture.

Next, we thought about our family legacy when considering our homeschool plans. What do you want your student to take away as part of your family heritage? My father was from Puerto Rico and I wanted Spanish and Latin studies to be a central part of my child's education. Music was an essential part of my husband and my childhood. Our hope was to encourage our student to develop a rich love and appreciation for music. We balanced all of our family dreams with our student's passions in history and science studies.

Don't make my mistake of trying to create public school at home. Be bold with incorporating elements which speak to your family's heart from educational dreams, legacy, and culture. Pass along passions that are important to your family. Invite your student to dream up their own desires for learning.

God gives us amazing freedom, which extends to our homeschool. We have the chance to make it a reflection of the unique family identity given by Him. Keep loves and legacy at the very heart of designing your education environment. Make your homeschool truly yours.

Think
What would a homeschool look like that is a true reflection of your family?

Starting Slow

"I have seen something else under the sun: The race is not to the swift or the battle to the strong, nor does food come to the wise or wealth to the brilliant or favor to the learned; but time and chance happen to them all." Ecclesiastes 9:11

A long time ago I ran a marathon. In Alaska. At the base of Mt. McKinley.

My husband-to-be and I were newly-engaged and we thought it was the perfect way to prepare for a lifetime together. What better metaphor for marriage could there be than training for the long haul of a marathon? It sounded like a good idea at the time.

One of the first things we learned about training for a marathon is to "start slow." The tendency of newbies is to get completely caught up in the excitement and frenzy of the marathon and start off too fast. This was true for me, too. On a beautiful June day with thousands of runners on the starting line, I felt like I was ready to conquer the world. By mile twenty, I only wanted to find a way to finish. Somehow.

I was coached by veterans to go slower at the start than what you know you can do. This way, you always have the energy in your tank to go faster as your momentum builds. This is a helpful way to think about the beginning of the homeschooling year. Starting slow feels like a kinder, gentler way to move into the school year.

After all, our schedules are changing from the relaxed pace of the summer season to the overfull calendars of academics, sports, lessons, and activities. It's important to go slowly and pace yourself, realizing this time of transition can be hard for everyone, not only your kids.

You may need to go slowly at first in organizing your day and setting up systems. Work together on calendars, scheduling the day, figuring out a system to make the day flow best. Have grace for yourself and your kids as you are setting up your process. Your family is learning how to become independent workers. Take the time to start well so that your kids learn good systems right from the beginning.

Coming from the freestyle flow of summer, getting into the habit of working diligently throughout the school day can be tough for everyone. In our home, we decided our brains needed a break after 45 minutes or so. It helped us to set a timer, then get up, move around, change rooms, do a chore. Another trick we used was to make time visible with a wall calendar to show the time available to study and for activities during the day.

Parents need to remember to take breaks and rest too. When I was running the marathon, I decided I would hydrate during the water stops every 5 miles. Planning rest in your school day is a nurturing help to fuel your week. Consider something fun to look forward to during your week like a park day with friends to celebrate the end of the week or a game night with family.

When I was running the marathon, staying positive kept me going. All along the race route, people were clapping and cheering my husband and I on. When I felt I couldn't go much longer, there would be positive faces or encouragers saying, "You got this!" or "Only half a mile to the next water station." If you start to get down on your homeschooling day, turn it around by finding ways to stay positive. Look for anything good to cheer about. There is always something to celebrate. Even if it's "No one cried today!" or "We didn't argue during math!" Find goodness everywhere and anywhere you can.

After the ease of summer, school schedules and workloads feel heavy. Give yourself permission to feel what you feel. Pray for God's grace to cover your family. Ask for energy, enthusiasm, and wisdom on how to keep going. Remember this may be challenging for a few weeks as you establish new rhythms at home. Life will get better as things fall into place and everyone gets used to the new schedule.

When I was training for the marathon, I held the vision of crossing the finish line with my husband. And we did. We held hands and loped exhaustedly across the line to a stadium full of cheering fans. We had done it and God had seen us through. I hold a similar vision for homeschooling. I know God will be faithful again. If I am faithful in the small everyday tasks, God will be faithful in seeing us through to the finish line.

Think
How can you start slow?

Homeschooling Like Jesus

"Have I not commanded you? Be strong and courageous. Do not be afraid; do not be discouraged, for the LORD your God will be with you wherever you go." Joshua 1:9

If Jesus taught only with a stick and sand, I don't have any excuses.

Early in our homeschooling years, I joined a learning community where I was able to tutor and pour into other kids. I loved the chance to help others along the path of learning, but the community had one rule: no technology.

Their thinking was if Jesus used only a stick and sand to carry His world-changing message to everyone, it was good enough for us. At first, I thought this was ridiculous. There were so many phone apps for learning, games for practice, and videos for teaching. The Internet was basically the best teacher on steroids. Or was it?

The more I had to rely on the "stick and sand" method, the more I realized they were right. If you step away from the screens, you have to think creatively. It required good conversations, dismantling an idea and putting it back together. It required patiently sitting with a concept and pressing into the uncomfortable place of not knowing.

At first, I loathed not having all the answers. As I learned to press into the not knowing and relying on Christ to guide me, the more fun things became. I'm not saying I showed up without a clue, but there were plenty of times I grappled with ideas and invited the kids to join me in the struggle.

As a parent at home, the "not knowing" place felt frustrating to me at first. However, if homeschooling has taught me anything, it's to slow down. If we don't understand, it's perfectly fine to camp out for a while in the not knowing. When my student would come to me frustrated saying, "I don't get this at all," I knew this was a chance to embrace the challenge.

When you rest in the not knowing, it's much like our faith. We have to do all we know how to do, but we also have to look to God to guide us, direct our path, and show us how to walk it out. If we were able to work out all our challenges quickly, easily and in our own flesh, we would have no need for a Savior. We would rely only on our own abilities and we would not walk by faith.

The first thing I encouraged my child to do when they came across something hard was to start with what they knew. Everyone knows at least something. Start there. Invite them to think about what they know first, however small.

Next invite them to re-read the problem together and make sure they understand every word. Usually, a lot of frustration is saved when they review what is being asked and understand it completely.

Lastly, invite them to break it down. Have them narrow down what kind of problem this is, what it is asking, and where they may have seen things like this before. Usually when you encourage your child to slow down, go back over things in a deeper way and drill down to specifically what the problem is, they are able to get clarity.

Jesus taught in a similar way. He kept things simple and He used basic tools. He asked good questions and was curious. What I learned from the "stick and sand method" was that there are many ways to see things and solve things. When I could surrender the notion of having it all figured out, it freed me to be in the moment and to be curious. By holding the "not knowing" lightly, it allows for grace to play with ideas, not get every answer right.

My encouragement is to try the Stick and Sand method when your kids get stuck. Make it a game. Do all you know how to do together. Play with the ideas. Have interesting conversations. Leave room for the Holy Spirit to show up. God is always faithful.

Think

How can you embrace "not knowing" and stay curious?

Do It Yourself

"And this is my prayer: that your love may abound more and more in knowledge and depth of insight, so that you may be able to discern what is best and may be pure and blameless for the day of Christ, filled with the fruit of righteousness that comes through Jesus Christ—to the glory and praise of God." Philippians 1: 9-11

If it doesn't exist in homeschooling, you can always do it yourself.

As with home improvement projects, homeschool projects have an authenticity only found when you created from scratch.

Over the years, we have undertaken all sorts of **DIY** experiences from cooking skills, amateur stock trading, recycling projects, writing workshops, renewable energy, and hydroponic farm studies. These might be fulfilled in as many ways as you dream up: a field trip, a meeting with an expert, a workshop, something we create, or an enrichment class.

I used to think high school classes had to be serious, intense, test-oriented, and measurable. After all, if you can't assign a grade and quantify how much a person learned, how good could it truly be? If it's going to be as good as real school, it must be tested to show how much we learned. Or does it?

Some of the most meaningful experiences we enjoyed in homeschooling had nothing to do with books or measurements. Usually they involved exploring a curiosity, chasing down a whim of an idea or learning about something that we were genuinely interested in. These types of things we wanted to learn purely for the sake of learning.

Granted, not everything we studied was because we loved it. Absolutely, there are certain things you have to do to check a box whether it's math, science, reading, or social sciences. Yet how you weave in special interests is completely up to you.

I remember the summer before my son was going to be a senior. I had the sudden realization that my child had never taken any personal finance classes. How was he ever going to function in society if he didn't know how to write a check, make a budget, learn about debt, loans, and basic finances?

Veteran homeschoolers taught me when you want to learn something, it is perfectly acceptable to create it yourself. That is exactly what I did. I found a solid video and workbook curriculum and recruited some like-minded moms and student friends. I picked a date workable for most everyone and I included dinner to make it a true fellowship. We rotated who brought dinner each week. The personal finance students loved the time to come together weekly in a relaxed setting, learn about personal finance, and best of all, eat.

Because we had never done this before, there were no expectations. I wasn't a whiz at personal finance. I learned as much as the kids did. We did it all for the love of learning and because we were genuinely interested in the subject. All of it was gravy.

Look for opportunities in your homeschool to follow your family's passions. Don't be afraid to create opportunities for their life toolkit before they finish high school. Even if you have to create it yourself, enrichment experiences for your student can be meaningful for everyone.

Passion always beats knowledge when pursuing something new. Being a humble beginner in any subject can be a wonderful place to explore together.

Think
Are there areas your family has been longing to learn about which are outside the normal school structure?

A Beautiful Ecosystem

"Every good and perfect gift is from above, coming down from the Father of the heavenly lights, who does not change like shifting shadows." James 1:17

In homeschooling, learning is an extension of life.

School isn't limited to the timeframe of Monday through Friday from 8 a.m. until 3 p.m. Learning doesn't have to stop because you ran out of time in your 45-minute period. Over the years, I have come to appreciate that our homeschool doesn't need to be defined by a building, a calendar or a clock.

At first, I was worried about what people would think if we read literature in hammocks outside. Would taking a tour of a newly-opened hydroponic farm serve as a science field trip? Did attending a free lunchtime concert to hear a classical quartet qualify as a music appreciation? Did learning how to cook dinner every Monday give my son anything valuable?

Yes to it all.

When I was able to embrace the freedom of the ecosystem, learning became a joy. Remember, your homeschool does not need to look like anyone else's experience. If you are having trouble breaking out of the traditional school mold, here are a few good questions to consider:

"What is your student curious about?"

"What are their hobbies, both academic and fun?"

"For the classes you currently have, what are some real-world examples, field trips, people, or experiences you could weave in over time?"

"What would help your student's current subjects come alive?"

As your student ages up in high school, it becomes harder and harder to take time away from school. They have more schedule demands with friends, school, career, work, getting ready for life after high school, or college. Even though they don't have ample amounts of spare time, try to make time for getting outside of your four walls.

Homeschooling as an ecosystem invites your child to become a lifelong learner. If they begin to see everything in their midst as a classroom, life becomes one big curiosity. They appreciate they can learn about anything, anywhere, and at any time. The hope is they won't be afraid of any subject because they are curious about life.

Learning this way allows you to approach education in high definition. It becomes a living, breathing, walking around experience for your family when it transcends the ordinary. These will be the days when learning comes alive for them. Even though it's difficult to break from the schedule, take time for learning experiences. They are homeschooling gold.

Think
How can you extend your student's natural passions and curiosities beyond traditional learning? How can you help their education come alive as you go?

The Power of Stories

"We will not hide them from their descendants; we will tell the next generation the praiseworthy deeds of the Lord, his power, and the wonders he has done." Psalm 78:4

Homeschooling allows me to be "uncool."

One of my favorite "uncool" homeschool things was reading aloud together almost every day. Sometimes this looked like reading a passage of scripture together over breakfast, or perhaps funny articles over lunch. Some years we would take a book and read a page a day for a year. In quantity, this wasn't a huge pile of books, but the connection time it offered more than made up for the number of pages.

To be clear, I'm not saying every homeschool parent needs to read aloud to their child in high school. However, I always found a captive audience over mealtimes. It's amazing what you can read together in five minutes over a peanut butter sandwich. Sometimes I would pick articles about difficult subjects like binge drinking, college temptations, drugs, or teen sex. Reading articles from wise sources allowed us to address hard subjects in ways that felt more open. It encouraged conversation starters and allowed us to discuss tricky topics as a family.

If I didn't feel like reading to my child, sometimes I would simply lay open a magazine article I wanted him to read in a place where he would see it. Or I would crack open a beautiful history book on a subject he was studying. By placing an enticing book or reading resource in an area where your child is eating or hanging out on a regular basis, you are also encouraging them to read on their own. This may not work all the time, but it was surprising to me how often it did.

Regardless of the amount, reading together was the golden thread woven through our homeschool years. On long car rides, we would get lost in a good audiobook or storytelling podcast. During the often-difficult emotions happening in the teen years, stories became a way we could connect. Even if both of us were locking horns, we could still find our way back through good stories.

When I started to realize the end of high school was in sight, I started getting serious about making a "Must-Read Before High School Is Over Book List." There are many lists out there of books every high schooler should read. While these resources are wonderful, make your book list a reflection of you and your family. Consider what you read and loved, what your family treasured, not necessarily what the world deems quality.

For our book list, I wanted my son to read important works of historical fiction, featuring integrity and strong character examples. Particularly, I wanted my son to have a myriad of examples of strong, Christian men of integrity over time. We also read many of the classic books I enjoyed from my younger years such as The Chronicles of Narnia series, Sherlock Holmes, Swiss Family Robinson, and The Phantom Tollbooth.

Books have the power to shape who our kids become. Be

intentional about choosing excellent books and stories to guide and shape your child's character.

Even if you have to be a bit stealthy by placing quality reading materials in their midst, do it. They may not adore you reading books to them. Do it anyway. Keep it short. Keep it interesting. This may mean you read small pieces together, slowly, page by page. However, you are able to weave books in your days, the time spent in connection of stories will be memories your family will treasure for years to come.

Think
How can you make books and stories part of your homeschool days?

No Homeschool Is an Island

"Therefore encourage one another and build each other up, just as in fact you are doing." 1 Thessalonians 5:11

Unlike golf and pole-vaulting, homeschooling works best in community. While you may be incredibly smart and have all the resources you need, surrounding yourself with encouragers, wise counselors, and friends is vital for the long-term journey. For your student, mentors who can pour into your child are equally essential for their growth.

I prayed God would place people on my son's path who could speak truth into his heart. As my child aged up in the high school years, my voice became less important to him. It wasn't that my son disregarded all I had to say. I simply understood his longing for others to speak wisdom into his heart.

As a parent, be intentional about finding allies who can pour into your children on the homeschooling journey. It would be wonderful if they were all Christians, but sometimes they are not. Finding people with strong integrity, values, and a willingness to pour into your child can be life-giving. As people come across your path who could be equippers, invite them to speak wisdom into your child's life.

In our busy days, people may not be aware of how your child struggles or areas where they need encouragement. I'm not encouraging you to ask people to prop up your student's ego. However, as people come across your path who may be an inspiration to your student, consider inviting them to be a wise voice in their life.

I asked my friend, Kevin, a pilot, to mentor my son and share what it's like to have a career in aviation. I asked my neighbor, Dave, to encourage my son to do hard things or share stories of what it was like for him in med school as he struggled in classes. I asked Pat, my son's hockey coach, to help my son learn where he could contribute best to the team. I asked my neighbor, Andrew, to share some ideas on wing design for my son's Science Olympiad airplane project. I invited Mary, my son's piano teacher, to share how music can be more than lessons and to encourage him to find joy in music.

My friend, Jane, said it best when she shared, "I want my children to know I'm not the greatest thing that will ever happen to them in this lifetime. I want my children to find other sources of inspiration and wisdom by surrounding them with excellent mentors and encouragers."

My hope is that you will find others to pour into your homeschool student. If you are lacking in encouragers for your family, ask God to plant equippers on your path. Seek out positive voices in your neighborhood, extracurricular activities, sports, and faith community. Look at your current homeschool situation and think about the encouragers who are currently on your path. If there are many, count yourself blessed and invite them to share their wisdom in a specific way. It is perfectly okay to be strategic about inviting others to nurture and foster the best in your child.

God invited us to be a part of the body of Christ because no one part could accomplish everything on its own. Help your child to see that there is an entire community of encouragers who want God's best for their life. Invite God to plant life-giving equippers on your child's path.

Think
How can you be intentional about inviting others to pour into your student?

The Saving Grace of Humor

*"You make known to me the path of life; you will fill me
with joy in your presence, with eternal pleasures at your
right hand." Psalm 16:11*

If you're going to homeschool, you might as well have
some fun.

One of my friends said her kids referred to her as "Darth
Vader." They called her this because every time she walked
into the school room, the kids claimed all she did was yell at
them or speak in a mean voice. Don't be like my friend, or at
least not all the time.

Part of me wishes homeschooling could be as sweet and
joyous as Julie Andrews singing about learning as in the movie,
Mary Poppins. I know homeschooling is not sunshine and rain-
bows every day. Yet, we don't have to live our homeschool
days so serious that it drains the life out of everyone and
everything.

A homeschooling year is a long time. Typically, it's about
185 days if your state follows most guidelines. The good news
is we can decide how we feel on all 185 of those days. We
certainly will have days we feel terrible, have colds, are moody,

stressed, or lacking sleep. We will have bad days. The best news is we have the power to choose how we handle those days.

There were a lot of homeschooling days that I was Darth Vader, too. My son was driving me crazy. He wouldn't do his work or he didn't care about doing a good job. Some days he was emotional and tired. At times, I was harsh, mean, critical, and negative toward him. But sometimes, in the midst of an angry moment, if I was smart, I could change my mind. I could find something humorous and ridiculous about the situation and crack a joke and smile. Suddenly, everything would change.

Maybe you're like me and tend to take yourself too seriously. Or maybe humor isn't easy for you to come by. Try being humorous anyway. Look up jokes on the internet. Have your smart speaker tell you the joke of the day. Find funny days like International Lumberjack Day and come to breakfast wearing your best flannel shirt. Or if your child has a big sporting event that evening, make sporty-shaped pancakes. I used to make my son a hockey-goal-shaped breakfast with eggs, bacon and a hole cut in the toast for a puck. I know it's goofy, but it made everyone laugh.

Homeschooling is a lot of work, but it can also be fun. Look for little daily ways to spark humor and joy with your child. They may think you are strange, weird, or a kook. At least no one can ever say homeschooling is boring.

Dance party breaks, funny jokes of the day, themed dinners, and odd holidays can all be part of your home-school's daily rhythms. Homeschooling is as serious as it needs to be, but there is plenty of room for fun, too.

Jesus certainly walked this earth with joy on His face. I think He would want us to live that way, too. The school year is long. Have fun with your homeschool student. As the parent, you set the tone for your school environment. Why not set a joyful one? Remember, enjoying the homeschool journey is allowed and appreciated by everyone.

Think
How can you weave simple, fun things into your homeschool rhythms?

Mix It Up

"The Lord your God is with you, the Mighty Warrior who saves. He will take great delight in you;" Zephaniah 3:17

When I first considered homeschooling, I listened to the audiobook, *For the Children's Sake*[1] over and over again. This homeschooling classic by Susan Schaeffer Macaulay inspired me to dream about what an education could be.

I loved Macaulay's vision for a sweet "cottage school" with short lessons and plenty of time spent outdoors, no matter the weather. Her emphasis on quality material, no "twaddle" or busywork, resonated with me. Her education mindset emphasized love of learning. I hungered for an experience like that for my child. Because Macaulay had created this model over and over again over time, I knew it would be possible for my family, too.

Even though I never followed the traditional Charlotte Mason approach she encourages, many of the parts of this style of education were undeniable. Excellent content, short lessons, time spent outdoors, learning with your hands through craft, chores, and play. All of these lovely elements were easy to get behind.

Certainly, these ideas are easier to put into place in the younger homeschool years. As we advance in high school, there is a lot of pressure to put academics into place that the "world" deems appropriate. Things like Honors or AP classes, community college experiences, or a boatload of extracurricular activities to make a world-worthy transcript. It's wonderful to pursue these things. Yet to remind myself why we were homeschooling, I needed to weave in some good stuff too.

When I say good stuff, I'm talking about enrichment that speaks to your child's heart and passions. What value is there in homeschooling if I was simply recreating the traditional learning experience at home? My encouragement is stay true to why you are on this journey by taking time to mix it up. As a high school schedule gets more demanding, this can be difficult. With a little creativity and planning, you can still find fun ways to keep learning vibrant.

During my son's sophomore year, we took a ski trip right in the middle of winter. It wasn't during a winter break from classes or a holiday break. It was smack dab in the middle of the week and required my son to plan his classwork appropriately. With permission from his instructor, he completed a portion of his work before we left. He committed to doing another portion of the work while travelling to the skiing destination. Then he attended live class in between ski runs. With a chance to mix skiing with learning, he was up for the challenge.

A friend of mine loved to plan high school field trips for a group of families. She organized a group of high school kids to attend cultural performances every month for a year. My son looked forward to the outings which always involved donuts afterwards, as well as seeing his friends. We would plan our work schedule accordingly in order to see friends, have fun and escape from the daily school grind each month.

Around the home, we try to have a huge puzzle happening

on a regular basis. We cook together every week, make bread together in the wintertime, and practice grilling together in the warmer months. My son loves to set up balsa wood projects in the garage so he can take a break to tinker, build, and design in the garage regularly.

We may not be living a school life in the dreamy English countryside surrounded by roaring fires, great books, and rambling fields. However, we can design a goodness-centered education matching our loves and dreams. Even though we have to follow some structures for what the world values, we can infuse our days with lovely pursuits. Homeschooling centered around loves reminds us not only of our true passions, but also the Creator who inspired them.

Think
How can you keep things fresh and vibrant in your homeschool in simple ways?

Trusting Yourself to Homeschool Well

*"No, in all these things we are more than
conquerors through him who loved us." Romans 8:37*

Believing in yourself is half the battle in homeschooling. Actually, it might be the only battle.

One of my all-time favorite movie scenes is from *The Wizard of Oz.* Near the end, Glenda the Good Witch tells Dorothy she could go home anytime she wanted. She informs Dorothy she had the power all along, she only needed to believe.

Homeschooling feels a bit like Dorothy's trip. We set off on the adventure not really knowing where we are heading. We search for truth and knowledge. We run into lions, tigers, bears, good, and bad things along the way. We face our fears and hopefully melt them. We plan to eventually get to the Emerald City for the approval stamp of knowledge. Then we find out, at the end, we knew what we were doing after all. We had the power all along on this journey. We simply needed to realize it.

In this light, homeschooling is more about listening to God and your own instincts than following the exact right path.

When I first started homeschooling, I wanted to do it "right." Yet the more I talked to different parents and learned about different styles of homeschools, I learned there is no "right" way to do it. There is only "our" way of doing things.

Homeschooling is a lot like parenting well. It starts with seeking God, trusting your instincts, and asking for help when you need it. It's more about believing you have everything you need and to trust in that. You know what to do, it's a matter of listening to the voice and doing it.

Everyone's homeschooling journey will look different. For our family, our priority was a liberal arts style education. For others, science and math were a greater priority. We liked beginning our days by 9 a.m., but I had many friends who didn't begin school until noon each day. We designed our school for things that were a fit for us. Some homeschooled with large families, others like mine where only with one child. Each has their own gifts and challenges. God gifted us all so differently to make our paths creative and interesting.

If you find yourself lacking confidence in what to do, pretend you already know. Listen to your heart and allow your wise self and God's direction to lead you. Your homeschool can be a lovely reflection of your unique life and situation. Sometimes this takes courage to dare to do things your own way.

This might mean taking breaks when you need it or when your kids need it. It might mean reading for an entire day or watching documentaries about World War II because your student wants to take a deep dive into history. Some days it means you spend time with family or running errands because a loved one requires it.

For me, it meant surrendering what the books said, what my friends were doing, and what traditional school looked like. When I could shut out all the influences and deeply listen to how God was directing me, it became clear what to do. I was able to plainly see what I knew needed to happen. I only needed the courage to listen and follow through on what was already there.

My encouragement is to follow your own heart. Ask God to direct your plans and to have the courage to follow them. Listen to the voice of love within, it never fails.

Think
How can you trust yourself and God with your homeschooling journey?

The Daily Walk
CHAPTER TWO

Inspiration and ideas to support the daily journey of homeschooling.

"Fix these words of mine in your hearts and minds; tie them as symbols on your hands and bind them on your foreheads. Teach them to your children, talking about them when you sit at home and when you walk along the road, when you lie down and when you get up." Deuteronomy 11:18-19

What is Your First?

"Whatever you do, work at it with all your heart, as working for the Lord, not for human masters." Colossians 3:23

How you begin your homeschooling day makes all the difference.

When I first started homeschooling, friends said, *"Make your homeschool soar by starting with chores!"* Initially I thought this was a cheesy idea, but soon appreciated the wisdom.

In my mind, chores were handled after we finished school-work at the end of the day. Typically, academics consumed most of our day before dashing out the door to sports, appointments, or get-togethers. Ultimately, chores were pushed to the weekends and often never.

I knew if I wanted my child to develop life skills and the habit of chores, I needed to make them a priority. At the beginning of the week, I typically gave my son a couple of chores to be done first thing in the mornings. Trash patrol, dog poop patrol, laundry, emptying the dishwasher, tidying his room. We agreed chores always needed to be done first so they wouldn't be forgotten in the chaos of the day.

The chores weren't anything strenuous or overly time

intensive. They were simple things which needed to be done each week. One year we instituted "Man Time Mondays." I wanted my child to learn how to cook and Mondays were the days he would make dinner for the whole family. Usually, the menu was something simple like pasta or tacos. He was in charge of it from start to finish.

On the weekends, more labor-intensive jobs were available, which I called, "Jobs for Hire." These were things I was willing to pay my child to complete and he enjoyed being rewarded for hard work. When he was saving for something or wanted extra money, he would ask me if there were any "Jobs for Hire." We didn't give our child an allowance, so these jobs became an opportunity to earn and contribute.

At first, I thought chores as part of the homeschool day seemed like a silly notion. When I began to see it differently, I realized we were training our child for service and obedience. As parents live under the authority of and in obedience to God, our children live under the authority of and in obedience to their parents. Our kids need the experience to contribute to the family. Chores are a meaningful way to accomplish this.

This may look different in your home. It's tempting to think their "work" is school and getting good grades, volunteering, service, and extracurricular activities. For me, it was important for my child to serve the home operation beyond doing schoolwork. If we remove service to the family, we rob our kids of the chance to develop important life skills. They need to know how to care for a home, their personal environment, and provide service to others. They need to practice the living example of service under God, parents, and family.

Yes, high school academics mixed with extracurricular activities, church, work, and social time can be a demanding schedule. Still our children need to know how to function as contributing, caring humans in the world. This starts with their daily walk at home. If you make it first, it gets done.

Chores set the tone for the day in your child's heart that everything isn't about them.

Yes, my friends were right, chores do make your homeschool soar. This wasn't just a cheesy tagline, but a helpful, practical way to serve as a good steward for all God has given our family.

Think
How will you encourage service to family as part of your child's homeschool day?

Loving Traditions

"Follow God's example, therefore, as dearly loved children and walk in the way of love, just as Christ loved us and gave himself up for us as a fragrant offering and sacrifice to God." Ephesians 5:1-2

What do you want your child to remember about the days of homeschooling?

When you are knee-deep in hard academics, transcripts, standardized testing, college/career choices, and meaningful extracurricular activities, it can be challenging to think beyond the moment. Yet the reality is one day your child will graduate and leave home. They will look back on these days you are walking through right now. What will you want them to remember?

I wanted my child to develop a rich faith with tiny deposits made over the long haul. I hoped for meaningful, thoughtful conversations to be the fabric of our days, whether it was woven by seeing God in scripture or in physics. My desire was to raise a thinking, curious, virtuous young man who wasn't afraid to learn anything and would follow God all the days of his life.

Your vision for what your student takes away from high school may look different from mine. However, my guess is we share the ambition of cultivating hearts and minds in the best possible way. How do you do that?

I think it starts by modeling it for them. We begin by being curious ourselves, reading interesting things, asking good questions, and creating space for our student to wonder about life. I think it starts with being intentional with your conversations and experiences on a daily basis.

High schoolers don't have a lot of time. If they do, they typically don't want to spend all of it with their parents. You have to be a bit sneaky with weaving in times of connection. Simple, intentional acts of care might be the loveliest things they will remember ten years from now.

My hope was to create memories as part of our days with seasonal rituals. Traditions to support your school year do not have to be expensive or complicated. It could be as simple as making homemade bread in a bread machine together and letting its aroma fill your home on a rainy fall day. It could mean spreading out a 1,000-piece puzzle on the table to work together as a family after dinner. Maybe it's a favorite seasonal movie and hot cocoa with popcorn. Traditions are about being intentional with how you connect as a family and may look different in every season. Find ways to nurture your child's heart as part of the journey.

As Christ loved us, we pour out this same love on a daily basis to put our faith in action. These small loving acts are what will create memories lasting long after graduation. They may feel like ordinary things, but they are the things that will make extraordinary memories for years to come.

Think
What simple, loving experiences can you weave into your homeschool week to bring your family joy?

Walking It Out

"*You will keep in perfect peace those whose minds are steadfast, because they trust in you. Trust in the Lord forever, for the Lord, the Lord himself, is the Rock eternal.*" Isaiah 26:3-4

Reading scripture shows me more of God. While I appreciate scripture's history, language, and rich storytelling, I long to know it in a deeper way. Mostly, I struggle with going from reading the Word to living the Word.

Lately, I have been searching for how to trust God more. I read about Paul in prison trusting God or Ezekiel surrendering his daily actions or Esther going to the king on behalf of the Jews. I read their stories and I am inspired by how they listened to God and walked out their faith with complete trust. I long for their ability to trust.

To simply say, "Trust God" sounds easy. I pray and ask for wisdom and I surrender my plans. Yet, I find myself anxiously doing and fretting and stewing over things anyway.

I see my son and I want him to get a summer job, to make plans for getting ready for the college season ahead. We discuss it and I make suggestions. I encourage him to move forward with these plans. We talk through the how-tos and what it looks like to make things happen. Then I wait.

As a parent, I have done all the things I know to do short of doing it for him. I know he needs to learn how to take responsibility for his life. I am trying to back off and create space for him to practice becoming an adult. If I do these things for him, I'm stunting his growth and forcing him to do them my way. I know I need to trust he will walk it out according to how God inspires him. I find it hard not to want to help or do it for him.

I think through the worst-case scenario of my son playing video games all summer or defaulting to his past summer job of working in fast food. I know this would not be the end of the world and I know God can use this, too. I have to trust that perhaps video games and fast-food employment are exactly what God has in mind to inspire my child to desire more for himself.

I know when I surrender my plans for my child, I create space for God to go to work with His plans. As a parent, my role is to do all I can to inspire God's best. Ultimately, how my child walks that out is up to him.

God's plans are higher than any I could ever imagine. I have to make space for God to show up. It starts with trusting Him with all of it.

Think
How do you walk out trusting God?

The Golden Hour

"Satisfy us in the morning with your unfailing love, that we may sing for joy and be glad all our days." Psalm 90:14

If you asked me my favorite thing about homeschooling, I would say, "Morning Time." The "Morning Time" idea is not new and was first shared by many veteran homeschoolers as a supportive framework for starting the day. What I loved most was the life-giving way this allowed us to connect each morning.

"Morning Time" is what my son and I affectionately called the first part of the day spent together over breakfast. It looked different in every season and at every age, but we made it a priority to have morning time, even if only for a few minutes.

For our morning time, we started our day reading the Bible. I'm not talking about huge amounts of reading. Sometimes it was only a page or a paragraph, and sometimes it was only one line. We dedicated ourselves to start the day in scripture, usually with a minimum of a couple sentences. We weren't Bible scholars, we were simply curious together.

After reading a few sentences, we would ask each other a

couple of questions. It was tempting for me to make this an academic exercise. Instead, I learned it worked best to keep it light, simple and short. As breakfast fuels the body, time in scripture and prayer fuels the heart and mind. After scripture, we talked about anyone in our circle who needed prayer that day. We asked God to direct our path. Sometimes I would pray and sometimes my child would pray if he was open to it.

Some days our morning time was as short as five minutes. Sometimes we would get caught up in a rich discussion and spend closer to thirty minutes. Be open to how God leads you. More than anything, don't miss this golden chance to connect with your kids.

How you begin the day is key. As parents, we have to be strategic to make the days meaningful. Everyone has to eat, right? If you think about it, you have a captive audience over breakfast. This is your chance to truly connect with your child as a way to start the day in the best possible way.

Lastly, you don't have to be a Bible wizard or have all the answers about scripture. Your student may not be a morning person, or your connection time is actually during lunch break. Find a timeframe that works for your family. They may not like it at first. Keep at it anyway. You only need to create space and intention to invite God to work. Help everyone start the day well by aligning your hearts and minds to our true north, our Savior.

Let your first hour of the day be the one that sets the tone for goodness in Him.

Think
How can you help start off your day well?

Worth It

"So that you may live a life worthy of the Lord and please him in every way: bearing fruit in every good work, growing in the knowledge of God." Colossians 1:10

Nothing pursued out of love will ever be lost.

When I began to think about how much I put into our homeschool season, I wondered if all of this effort would be worth it. Was it truly worth pouring every ounce of myself into my kids' education?

Certainly, with everything there is a cost. With this time, I could be working, bringing home more money, and buying more stuff. I would have better hair, nicer clothes and enjoy a lot more lunches with girlfriends. Most likely, I would exercise more and have more time for coffees, shopping, errands, and "me" time.

When I compare those things to the bigger vision, they feel hollow. For me, the long-term view holds the things I call "homeschool gold." Things such as hearing my son pour out his heart on what he thinks about a subject. Gold also might look like sharing an audiobook together and having rich conversations about the story and characters. As a homeschool parent, I have the opportunity to guide my child's heart on a daily basis, or at least be available to do so. When I think about it in this way, there is no comparison.

While you are in the homeschool years, it's not wrong to miss things you enjoyed before this season. It's perfectly fine to have nice clothes, spend time over coffee with girlfriends, or have "me" time. It's wonderful to sprinkle those into your schedule. If you are smart, you will still find a way to weave those into your life.

When I'm discouraged, I pile on all the reasons why this season stinks. My child hates this. I hate this. Why are we making ourselves miserable? If he attended regular school, I would have time to clean, cook, and exercise. I would be a better wife, a better mom, a better everything.

Maybe. Or maybe I need to give myself some grace. Perhaps I need to simplify, slow down, delegate, do less, put my phone down, or stop looking at social media. Quite possibly if I am struggling, it could be a character issue, mine or my child's.

Homeschooling magnifies our strengths and our weaknesses. Not only do I facilitate classes like algebra and British literature, but also unexpected subjects like my pride, ego, perfection, and approval issues. In homeschooling, you will have to look at your own stuff and you might not like it.

But our God is big enough to handle it. I trust He has amazing plans for my family. I believe deeply and unequivocally this pursuit is worth it.

Even if we decide not to homeschool beyond this year, month or week, the time spent walking alongside my child with loving intentions will never be lost. God will use all of it to serve me and my family. He will do the same for you.

Walk in a manner to show your family that homeschooling is worth it. Trust that your child and your family are worth it.

Know deep in the places in your heart that your God is more than worth it, because He is.

Think
How can you trust in the knowing that your efforts are more than worth it?

Holding Things Loosely

"Commit to the LORD whatever you do, and he will establish your plans." Proverbs 16:3

Checklists are my jam. I am a pencil-and-paper-style person and seeing the day laid out before me helps me feel calm and organized. To me, order means lovely pauses for rest and breathing room in my day.

My child does not like order. He likes technology and getting lost in a subject and tinkering and mess and chaos. He likes piles and leaving things to come back right where he left off.

When we would check in about weekly plans, I would put a paper calendar in front of him and ask him to map out his schedule. He would kindly oblige for a week or two and then it would quickly fade away. For him, it felt like wearing clothing that was two sizes too small. Having an endless weekly calendar staring at him was overwhelming. It was a reminder that he had a long way to go in the school year.

Ultimately, we would both end up frustrated. I would be angry that he couldn't see the wisdom in my orderly style. He would be discouraged because he thought his plans were never good enough in my eyes. With lots of passive-aggressive sighing, we would both walk away from our planning time resentful of each other's viewpoint.

In the end, I had to let it go because it was compromising our relationship. I could tell it was setting the tone for the day with a gloomy cloud over both of us. Holding my plans loosely and allowing him to do it his way was life-giving to him. I didn't arrive at this decision from a wise, virtuous place. Truly, it was from an exasperated, "I give up" sort of place.

What happened next was remarkable.

For planning, he decided to use a big wall-sized white board. He enjoyed the physical experience of writing his plans for the day in large words, which helped him stay focused. He would make a list of the things he wanted to accomplish for the day, and he felt extremely gratified when he got to check them off. He loved it so much, he even began mapping it out in time increments, scheduling in breaks, snacks, and chores. It became far more focused, detailed, and prioritized than I could ever fathom.

When I was able to surrender my plans or at least hold them loosely, it allowed my child's true style and personality to bubble up. He took ownership of the experience because it was his own. He loved it and poured more into it than anything I could ever ask him to consider.

Having grand plans for your student and guidelines for how things should be done is perfectly okay. However, being willing to let those go for your child to move in ways that inspire them is also important. Be free in knowing God has made our children unique versions of Himself. Allow your child the grace to pursue how they go about the day in their own style. Yes, give them guidance, strive for excellence, and pursue things in a manner worthy of our Creator. But more importantly, hold your plans loosely to see how God inspires them.

Give your child the gift of knowing you trust them to let

their path be their path. They have to know you believe in them enough to try things their way, even if their way looks different from yours. In fact, their way might be amazing.

Think
How can you hold your plans loosely to allow more of your child's personality to shine?

The Secret Sauce of Road Trips

"I have told you these things, so that in me you may have peace. In this world you will have trouble. But take heart! I have overcome the world." John 16:33

Long car rides might be the secret sauce for connecting with your child.

When I was going through a particularly rough patch with my teenage son, my friend Sally suggested taking a road trip. At first, I thought this was strange advice, but she was right.

There is something about riding side-by-side, both eyes forward in car which allows the space and freedom for your child to open up. Having an opportunity to truly connect is vital for parents. This is especially true during the teen years when emotions run high and a simple, "How are you?" can come across as a loaded question.

Susan was brilliant when she suggested a road trip. The journey doesn't have to be far, but trips can be a wonderful chance to come together with your child. Travelling with your child may be educational, career exploring, cultural or fun. There are so many travel opportunities in high school with college visits, concerts, museums, or an activity related to your child's passions. Set an intention to spend some time away with your child as a way to pour into your relationship.

I remember driving home from a time in the mountains with my son. Somehow, we wandered onto the topic of college applications and plans for the future. I asked my child how he was feeling about the whole process as it was unfolding. Then I did a miraculous thing, I shut up and listened.

My son poured out what was on his heart. He shared how much he doubted his abilities. How he saw older family members that had it together and how he could never be like them. He talked about how his dad and I appeared to be perfect people and that he was sure to disappoint us. He felt inadequate when he compared himself to all of his peers, who came across so much smarter than he was. He was unsure he could do college well.

My son was right, and he was wrong. In the position from where he sat, it did appear that his dad and I had it all together. What he didn't know is how much we, as parents, struggle too. He didn't see how many mistakes we still make all the time. He didn't know how much all his friends and family members, myself included, have to wrestle with constant doubts and fears. I assured him none of us are perfect people, but we can trust a perfect Savior.

From that day on, I reminded myself my child needed to see my examples of failures, equally as much as the successes. What he needed to see was that we mess up often and we have to seek forgiveness from God and from each other.

Our children need us to show them what it looks like to make mistakes, ask forgiveness, and move forward. They need to know their parents are human and still have doubts and fears about life. They need to see our model what to do with those screw ups, doubts, and fears by giving them to God and asking for forgiveness.

Homeschooling well isn't simply picking out academics, courses, books and activities. All of those things are important.

The richer, deeper education is how we are encouraging our kids and families to follow hard after Jesus all of the days of their life. It is important to show them how you struggle with difficult things, yet still seek the Lord's face. Our kids need to know we are not perfect people, but we serve a perfect God.

Think
How does your child see you? How can you model authenticity in your family today?

Thinking Small

"Are not five sparrows sold for two pennies? Yet not one of them is forgotten by God. Indeed, the very hairs of your head are all numbered. Don't be afraid; you are worth more than many sparrows." Luke 12:6-7

Some is better than none.

This expression is one of my favorite pieces of advice. It works well with most everything -- exercise, chocolate, money, and even homeschooling. On the days when no one is motivated to get started or to face a daunting paper, I encourage my child to think of one small thing he can do.

When I struggle with how to work on a hard thing, I have to trick myself. Instead of thinking about this big, hairy thing that looms heavily over me like the Abominable Beast in my face, I think about the smallest of small thing I can do.

For example, with exercise, typically I think about how long this will take and how much I have to do and I don't have time for this. I am trying to change my mind to think small. I think, "Just walk for five minutes" or "Just walk to the end of the street." When I can divert my focus from the reasons why this is hard to staying present to putting one foot in front of the other, then the walk happens. I start noticing the sky, the birds, and the neighbors' pretty yards and then I am lost in the quiet of hearing my own breath. The walk gets done.

The same goes for algebra, group projects, college essays, or things that are hard for your student. Invite them to do the smallest thing to move forward, even if it's only for five minutes. Sometimes you may need to come alongside them for encouragement. When my son was completing college applications and essays, I sat beside him. It was hard for him. He lacked confidence. He needed to be able to ask questions easily or verify he was doing it correctly. Sometimes your student may need help breaking it down into the smallest of increments.

Each day I want to choose better. I want to be better at health, time management, encouragement, loving my family, practicing my faith. My hope is by putting "some" of the better in place every day, I'm working toward the very best Jesus has for me. I wish I could say I always get it right and don't choose the things I shouldn't. With grace, I look for small ways to get back on track daily.

Homeschooling well is all about the tiny, good things accomplished consistently over time. If I can look for good-ness in the smallest things, I can move myself forward. By choosing to do this one day well, I'm faithful to Him. My hope is that these daily choices ultimately lead to finding God's best. To discover that, I must be a good steward in the small things first.

Think
How can you choose to honor God in the small things today?

Savoring

"Remember this: Whoever sows sparingly will also reap sparingly, and whoever sows generously will also reap generously." 2 Corinthians 9:6

What habits fill your day?

The word "habit" can feel heavy at times. It reminds me of hard things such as eating vegetables, exercising every day and being disciplined in my efforts. Habits remind me of all the things I "should" be doing, not things that come naturally.

Recently, I heard an idea that changed my mind about habits. It invited me to think about "savoring a new habit." I love the word "savor." The idea of savoring brings to mind a delicious meal, watching a sunset, enjoying a good piece of cheese or a slice of pie. Savoring was an idea I could get behind.

Whether we want to admit it or not, habits affect more than our own lives. Our kids are watching our habits. Even though they hide out in their bedrooms and we may think they care more about their cell phone than us, they see us and our habits.

Looking back over the prior day, I considered what my

habits said about me. I saw myself as a mom glued to technology, responding to text messages and emails like it was a competitive sport. I saw myself as a parent, so busy and checklist oriented, I was only half present to conversations. I saw someone who put accomplishing as the first discussion of the day. Then later in the day, I gave my family the tired and cranky mom, barking orders of chores, hurry-up demands for dinner, and naggy reminders. The worst habits of all showed up at the end of the day. The habit of being an escape artist, numbing out on television or a glass of wine to decompress from a long day.

I could do better. The habits I was modelling were not what I wanted for myself or my child. Instead of what I was unintentionally modelling, what opportunities did I have to choose better for myself and my family?

For me, I had to start small with "savoring a new habit." Instead of a glass of wine, I chose a nice herbal tea. Instead of television all the time, I decided I would pick up a good book, take a hot bath, or go to bed earlier. For technology, I am still working on that one. A good place to start is with no phones at mealtimes and putting my phone on silent while talking to people to show I am fully with them.

I know it's going to take some time to embrace new habits. However, instead of changing for my own personal benefit, I can see the higher calling. My daily walk is equally as important as the words I use. I can show my child what a parent working toward wholeness looks like. I can choose differently and better. I can choose to find new habits to savor in Christ.

Think
What is one new habit you can savor?

Upgrading

"For this very reason, make every effort to add to your faith goodness; and to goodness, knowledge." 2 Peter 1:5

Upgrades are nice when it comes to air travel, hotel rooms, or wardrobes. Those upgrades are something I want to do. Upgrades are hard when it means change and re-thinking the way we operate as a family.

Lately, I've been considering upgrading with the questions I ask. Usually, I ask the same things like, "How was your day?" or "Did you get your homework done?" or "Did you do your chores?" Then I am constantly irritated when I get the same answers of "Fine. Yes. Almost."

Upgrading my questions needed to start with upgrading my thoughts. What did I truly want to understand with those questions? Was I projecting worry, fears, or nagging onto my child? Did I want to hear about the day or was I running through my usual script? Was I available for meaningful conversations?

Typically, I was not. Usually, I was somewhere between a bunch of emails, doing laundry, making dinner, running errands, and unloading the dishwasher. Why would anyone want to have a conversation with me when I wasn't even there in the first place?

I wanted to ask better questions. I wanted to get better answers. I wanted to have more meaningful connections as a result. How was I to start? What is the best question a parent can ask their child on a regular basis?

If you are like me, you have probably been asking terrible questions for years thinking you were only making conversation. I didn't even know I was a terrible question asker in need of reform. To begin, I decided to simply ask my child. Friends shared early on in homeschooling that my child would become one of my greatest teachers. Well, here we are.

I asked my son, "What are better questions I can ask about your life that are encouraging and that you would like to hear?"

Here's what he suggested:

"What's your plan for the day?" (for schoolwork and chores)

"Do you have anything fun planned this week?" (for social, friends and fun)

"What's the funniest thing that happened today?" (for connection)

If nothing funny happened, you can always substitute, weirdest thing, coolest thing, interesting thing, where you saw God at work today, and so on.

Your child might have different questions they would like for you to ask. Ask them for good questions to find out how they are doing and what is happening in their world. It feels obvious to ask our kids about meaningful ways to connect with them. Still, I am guilty of forgetting to ask the obvious things.

The high school years are strange days, but they are fleeting. Your child is slowly transforming into an adult right before your eyes. The way you talk to them, interact with them, and encourage them needs to transform with your days. Having meaningful connections with them is an upgrade that doesn't cost anything. It only requires that you ask.

Think

How can you upgrade the way you communicate with my child? What are better questions you can ask them?

The Power of Our Words

*"Do not let any unwholesome talk come out of your
mouths, but only what is helpful for building others
up according to their needs, that it may benefit those who
listen." Ephesians 4:29*

What do your words say about you?

Words are something we use all day. We use them when
we talk to each other, when we write emails, when we make
phone calls, and even in our minds when we talk to ourselves.

Every morning, I noticed the first words I spoke to my
family were always about productivity. I am an early riser and
I usually get up hours before others gather in the kitchen.
Because I'm already in work mode, I sometimes forget to wish
them good morning and ask how they are before launching
into the most important tasks for the day.

Realizing this, I decided to pause. Were my words were
giving life to my family or were they making them feel put
upon? Does reminding my son to do his laundry take away
from the chance for him to experience independence?
Certainly, dirty laundry and the consequence of having no
clean clothes allows for life to be the teacher.

Or if I'm nagging my husband to make time to complete my honey-do list this weekend, is that bringing us closer as a couple? Perhaps there is a better, lighter way to share these things.

I know things need to happen around the house. Does my constant reminding add joy to the situation? Probably not. Is there a way to communicate that doesn't drain those around me? How can I foster building up my family?

With my son, we usually aimed for a Monday morning meeting during which he would share important plans, assignments, and activities for the week. These were key times to talk about important chores that needed to be completed, at his discretion. This was my chance to review things like laundry, tests, appointments, and other priorities. After that, no more discussion was needed. Life needed to be the teacher for missed assignments, dirty clothes, or consequences for not following through.

I learned that my husband loved it when I made a list for him and then gave him the freedom to complete it when he had time. This way he didn't feel pressured to do it according to my demands. It became like a fun challenge for him to get things done before his Saturday window to play golf with friends. Upon completion, it became his "free hall pass" to go play without guilt or burden.

As parents, we set the tone for the state of our homes and homeschools. Our words are the tool we can use to set a vibrant mindset for our families. We all say things we regret and not every conversation goes according to plan. Being aware of how words cultivate our family might be the single most powerful thing we do.

Use your words to give grace, healing, and sweetness to those we love, including ourselves.

Think

Where can you bring forth more of Christ in the words you use today?

Showing Up Anyway

"And hope does not put us to shame, because God's love has been poured out into our hearts through the Holy Spirit, who has been given to us." Romans 5:5

Embracing failure sounds like an important character experience, except when it's your own kid.

For several years, I coached a homeschool Science Olympiad team of students. Every season, right before competition, I would always receive a flurry of parent emails about their students. Desperately, parents would explain they couldn't possibly put their kids in a situation where they aren't prepared or will fail miserably. They ask to be removed from the team. They share all the reasons why they haven't been able to live up to their commitment and they always have excellent reasons.

I get it. Life happens. People get sick, family members need more from us, jobs change or go away. Life can be really hard at times. I'm not saying there isn't a time when it makes sense to cut your losses. Sometimes situations require us to quit, step away, or take breaks. This is the reason we homeschool. We pursue homeschooling to make it work best for our own family in the season of life we are living.

However, when we try to shield our kids from failure, we do them a disservice. We don't allow them the opportunity to develop the grit, tenacity, and strength they need for life. The lessons of failure give our kids many important tools. Our kids might need to see what it looks like when others succeed despite hard circumstances. Perhaps our kids will learn that, quite often, life is about showing up anyway and doing the best you can.

This idea is the heart of the homeschooling journey: to keep showing up and doing the best you can, day by day, little by little. The circumstances for having a chaos-free and stress-free life will never come. There will always be something to deal with, whether it's finances, sick family members, job insecurities, resources, time, energy, or faith. We will never homeschool in a perfect world. We have to ask God to carry us, especially when things are hard.

For my Science Olympiad parents, I give them a hug, I tell them I understand, and then I ask them to show up anyway. We get points for writing our names on a test or showing up at an event. They help our team simply by being there and being present. I invite them to take the pressure off, have grace, and support their team. In their state of utter imperfection, I ask them to show up anyway.

As parents, we need to be reminded there are life points for showing up anyway. Some of the best life lessons learned from homeschooling weren't the ones learned where my kid did everything perfectly. Typically, they were the lessons learned when my child was out of his league, lacking the preparation, and showed up anyway. Sometimes he got lucky, but mostly it was a lesson in accepting failure with grace.

My friend Tessa is a college professor in Toronto and shared with me the lesson of failure might be the most critical factor in whether kids succeed in life. She said about halfway through a freshman student's first semester of college it becomes painfully obvious who the kids are that have struggled a bit in life. She said it's difficult to watch the kids that have never had to find it in themselves to press through, to fail, and overcome. They lack confidence in themselves and their abilities because they have never been tested by failure.

Every fiber of me understands how hard it is to watch your child fail. I have been there many times. I still continue to watch my child fail. Yet, I have to keep reminding myself that we serve a big God who will carry us through. I trust in Him to know that failure is never final and will ultimately serve our family.

Think
How can you find a way to be let your child fail at times?

The Little Things

"Rejoice always, pray continually, give thanks in all circumstances; for this is God's will for you in Christ Jesus." 1 Thessalonians 5:16-18

People always say little things mean a lot. However, I think little things might be everything.

When you think about the big things -- weddings, once-in-a-lifetime family vacations, getting college acceptance letters, promotions, or big-deal birthdays, they come around only rarely.

Through little things, we are given the opportunity to find joy daily. There are so many tiny things which give me joy -- a good meal, how I feel after exercise, a scripture that feels like God is speaking to me personally, funny texts from friends. With small things, there are so many opportunities to find God's goodness in each day.

I think homeschooling well is about tiny things. Day by day, week by week, with intention and dedication we do the things that need to be done before us. Sometimes it's with ease and other times with difficulty. We can approach each day saying, "What small things do I need to do today?" In this way, the small things build up to the big things of learning, good habits, and a quality rhythm of consistency.

There are many days when I don't want to do the small things. The good small things like drinking more water, turning off mindless television shows, or stopping the endless scrolling through social media. Doing the small things requires paying attention. When I start to get tired, it's usually because I'm thinking of homeschooling every day for the rest of my life. I have to return to thinking about the little things. I change my mind to think: "Only for today, what things need to get done?"

Sometimes it requires tricking myself or my child when it's about things I don't want to do. If I have something hard to do or my student is struggling, I encourage them to think about what they can do. Can they work on it for 15 minutes? Can they watch a video that helps with the concept? Can they email a friend about working through it together? Can they reach out to the professor or class leader to ask for help? What small actions can help them accomplish difficult tasks?

Looking back on my years of homeschooling, it's the small things I remember. The vital, lifegiving things like spending time in the Word over peanut butter toast. The groaning and complaining from my son while learning how to cook on Man Time Mondays. The times when we would have interesting conversations about history, faith, or politics. My son's love of daily checklists and scheduling his day down to the minute on a huge whiteboard. The reading of books together and the places we travelled in the stories. These are only a few of the small things woven together into the fabric of rich, beautiful memories.

As you walk out this day, my encouragement is to think small. How can you be faithful with the small things God has placed before you? Take time to see, deeply see, the ordinary joys as God's blessings along the way, all for you.

<u>Think</u>
How can you honor God in small ways today?

Becoming

"You, God, are my God, earnestly I seek you; I thirst for you, my whole being longs for you, in a dry and parched land where there is no water." Psalm 63:1

In homeschooling, I was sure of what I wanted the end to look like. I imagined a strong, confident, virtuous young man who was passionate, curious about life, and following hard after Jesus all the days of his life.

In my heart, I believed if we got Jesus right, everything else would work itself out. This didn't mean everything would be easy. However, I knew a heart aligned to Christ would set a course for goodness.

The long-term vision and hope were easy to see. Yet I wondered how that worked on a Wednesday in the dead of winter? How do we live out virtue, passion, curiosity, goodness, and following hard after Jesus daily? Not easily.

The big vision of homeschooling felt good, but heavy. Would we ever get there? Would my unruly, moody, grumbly, and sweat-smelling teenager ever arrive at the virtuous young man stage? Would I ever arrive to the place of knowing what I was doing? Or would I always feel like I do now -- tired, chaotic, and stressed?

The end was easy to dream, yet I couldn't see the path to take us there. I clung to the promise that God would be faithful in filling in the gaps. Instead of focusing on the big things, I knew I had to focus on how I was living each day. I needed to look at the things I was surrounding myself with and who I was becoming on this journey. How was I modeling becoming more for Christ?

I am not a perfect person and I like junky stuff as much as the next person. However, if I'm going to encourage my child to do hard things, I needed to ask myself, "What hard things was I doing?" If I looked at my day, how was I becoming more for God and for my family?

Short answer, I wasn't. It's so easy for me to see the faults in others and in my own family, and yet not see my own short-comings.

I can nag my son all day long about making good choices such as being kind to others or loving people with a heart of grace. But if he sees me having a glass of wine to cope with stress, snapping at my family for not picking up after them-selves, or escaping away from the family, what am I really saying?

We all sin and fall short of the grace of God. Yes, I can make better choices to find ways to glorify Him in my actions. I know that it's not only choosing better for myself, but it's also about the ordinary ways I'm influencing my family.

I want to become more for God. I want to inspire my family to find more of Him too. My hope is to contribute more of God's goodness in our home. I may not always get it right, but with the heart of intention, I put myself in the posi-tion to become more for Him.

Think

How are you influencing your family to become more for God?

Bolder

"Be strong and courageous. Do not be afraid or terrified because of them, for the Lord your God goes with you; he will never leave you nor forsake you." Deuteronomy 31:6

Being bolder in Christ should be easy for me.

If I believe the Bible to be true, then I know Jesus freely died for my sins and by following Him, I get to spend my life in heaven. He loves me beyond compare and gives us the Holy Spirit to infuse our days with His grace and mercy. Why then, is boldly sharing my faith so difficult?

Some bold things are easy for me. Many people look at homeschooling and see it as a supremely bold choice. In some ways it is, yet in other ways it is easy. Because it was pursued out of a place of desperation and love, it became the easy choice.

I have bold friends who ask their waiters or waitresses how they can pray for them. They share their faith as easily as breathing. They ask the grocery store clerk for their prayer concerns or they invite their neighbors to church all the time. I wish these behaviors came easy to me.

Recently, the grocery bagger was walking my groceries to the car with me. I felt a tug on my heart to ask her how I could pray for her. I was tired, in a hurry, and in truth, I didn't want to ask her if I could pray for her. I was lazy and intimidated. I chickened out.

What was I afraid of? Was I afraid that the grocery bagger would be mad at me, that I would offend someone, or that the person would handle my groceries differently now that she knew I was a Christian? The grocery bagger girl was sixteen years old and I was scared to ask her how I could pray for her. I could do better.

My prayer has been to be bolder in Christ. I think Christ wants more from us than just reading the Bible, praying for people in our quiet time, and being nice people. There are plenty of nice people that are not Christians. My prayer is to be bold in the tiny, seemingly insignificant opportunities that come across my path. I pray that God will inspire me to share my faith everywhere I can.

I want to be a living, breathing, walking- around, life-giving Jesus follower. I don't want Jesus to be someone I only think about in my quiet time. Jesus isn't only discussed on Sunday mornings when I'm dressed up and have my Christian face on. I want to be a Jesus follower on a Tuesday afternoon in a grocery store parking lot.

If I truly want to be transformed in the renewing of my heart and mind as Jesus calls us to, I need to act differently, speak differently, live differently, and love differently. I need to be the walking-around church, not sitting in a seat and thinking about Jesus style church.

I think homeschooling helps us with this boldness. We have already made a bold choice, even though at times it feels like simply the next right thing to do. We are already living and operating counterculture from the world. To that end, it's not a difficult extension to think about using all we do for the love of Jesus.

My invitation is to think about where Jesus might be asking you to boldly put your faith in action. Maybe it's in grocery store parking lots or loving on a neighbor or encouraging a friend. I want people to know that I'm not only a nice person. I want people to know unequivocally that my love pours out from the hope I have in Jesus. All I do is because He loved me first.

Think
How can you put more boldness for Jesus in your day?

Unproductivity

"And we know that in all things God works for the good of those who love him, who have been called according to his purpose." Romans 8:28

As certain as the sunrise, there will be unproductive days.

My first response to an unproductive day is frustration. Because homeschooling is so efficient, it's easy to be discouraged by days that don't have much to show for themselves. After all, our kids literally have to flop out of bed, walk to the kitchen table, and they are in school.

Why can't I simply roll with the ebbs and flows of productivity? Instead, I start thinking, "the thoughts." The thoughts are the mean comments playing in my mind about what is truly happening here. My mean thoughts sound like this:

"If my child was in school, he wouldn't be so far behind in math."

"If he went to a real school, the technology would work all the time and be far superior to what you have."

"You are letting him goof off too much and now he is never going to make it into any sort of college."

"In fact, he will probably never leave the house and will be working a dead-end job and living in the basement."

When those voices come, I need to remind myself to take a deep breath. Every traditional school has days that are less than productive. Regular school calendars are sprinkled with teacher workdays, early release days, fire drills, active shooter drills, assemblies, changing classes, movie days, parties, and more. Even under the best of circumstances, no school is productive all the time.

If unproductivity is your norm, there may be a deeper problem. When this is the case, you may need to do some deeper evaluation and determine if the unproductivity is more of a character issue. These scenarios may require stronger boundaries for both parents and students to put more struc-ture in the day. This is not the sort of unproductivity I'm talking about.

I'm talking about the day that doesn't go as planned, when things are not getting done as hoped or something else is getting in the way. These days can also be part of the learning process too.

Remember, life happens. When things disrupt the normal flow and productivity of a day, how does your student handle it? How do you handle it? Can you use it as an opportunity for your student to problem solve instead of freaking out?

When the day gets derailed, have grace for both yourself and your student. It's okay to say, "Wow, that didn't go as planned. Let's make tomorrow a better day." Talk it through with your student and invite them to strategize about how things might need to happen differently tomorrow.

Most importantly, remember life is an excellent teacher. Walking side by side with your student through the ups and downs of life is as important as mastering Algebra 2. The hijackers of your day and unproductivity will come. Give yourself grace to know that this also is learning.

Think

How do you handle it when your day doesn't go as planned?

Embracing the Grind

"Finally, brothers and sisters, whatever is true, whatever is noble, whatever is right, whatever is pure, whatever is lovely, whatever is admirable—if anything is excellent or praiseworthy—think about such things." Philippians 4:8

Half of the challenge of doing hard things is the way we think about them.

This year, a friend motivated me to try working out in a class called High Intensity Interval Training or "HIIT" as it is fondly called. If you have never done this before, it's basically like a middle school gym class on steroids. Imagine heavy ropes and running laps around the building mixed with cardio, weights, and more crazy unimaginable things. I never thought I was capable of exercising this way. Yet I have grown to love the challenge, community, and intensity of the workouts.

To be honest, this style of workout is hard. I mean really hard. If you are doing it right, you pretty much feel as though you are dying the entire time. Then suddenly it's over and you feel like a million bucks not only for the hard work you did, but the accomplishment of it all. There are days when I'm jazzed to go work out, but there are more days when I'm dreading it.

I start thinking thoughts like:

"I don't know if I can do this."

"All the people here are younger and fitter than I am."

"I definitely can't do this."

"This is more than I can't handle."

My favorite instructor Kelly offers encouraging words during our warm-up. She motivates us with positive thoughts to change our thinking from dread to focus. Here's what she shares:

"Set your mind right."

"Clear all your thoughts away."

"You came to work. Get ready for it."

"Set an intention to work hard for these dedicated 45 minutes."

"You are so strong."

In the spaces of these encouraging words, I focus on my breathing. I make them my words and I suspend the doubting voices for a little while. I concentrate on the music or how I'm feeling in the moment. I think about completing the next five reps well, then the next five, then five more, and then I'm finished.

It strikes me as funny how influenced we are by our intentions and our thoughts. This mindset is same as it is for homeschooling: when we set our minds right, everything goes well.

When we are getting ready to work hard at our homeschooling day, we have to align our hearts and minds with Jesus. We set our intentions to work hard for Him. We lay down and wash away those doubting thoughts, cranky attitudes, and critical hearts. We focus on the breath our Creator gives us, and the profound love He has poured out for us.

Now when I wake up to go work out, most days I don't even allow myself to think about it. I know it's the purposeful, good thing that I'm choosing to do for myself today. Like brushing my teeth or showering, I don't think about it because I know it's what is next for my day.

Like caring for our bodies, homeschooling in this day we are given is also our purposeful good thing. We choose to set our minds on things above and allow our intentions to guide us in love.

If everything we do is considered an act of worship, homeschooling is an opportunity for a holy daily grind. We have the ability to set our minds to embrace this work with grace, love, and goodness.

Think
How can you set your mind with the best intention for your day?

Navigating Changes

"But because of his great love for us, God, who is rich in mercy, made us alive with Christ even when we were dead in transgressions—it is by grace you have been saved."
Ephesians 2:4-5

Every day is a chef's surprise when you homeschool a teenager.

Some days your high schooler will want your opinion and your brilliance on life. Other days they are annoyed at the sound of your breathing. Navigating the many moods and weather of a teenager is forever interesting. My hope is to foster God's goodness through all of it.

It's hard to stay grounded when your teen gives you attitude, drama, or defiance. Despite their sometimes-prickly outward appearance, they still need you, but they may need you in different ways. They are trying to grow up and become more independent, and they desperately want your respect. This doesn't always come across in obvious ways.

For parents, this may feel like solving a daily mystery. For the most part, we are staying the same and every day they are waking up trying to figure themselves out. Later in their high school years, they have the added stress and pressure of difficult classes, relationships, and figuring out what they are going to do after high school. All the while, they get a swath of new hormones, too.

As a parent, trying to figure this out is a bit like emotional whiplash. The same things I had done day after day, suddenly became overbearing and controlling. Alternately, I give more freedom and grace by backing off, and my child says I'm abandoning them and don't care.

Well, huh.

There is no magic answer here for how to navigate the changing relationship with your teen. That being said, staying prayed up, spending time in the Word, and having some time of quiet before the day begins is vital. Also, setting aside a regular time of devotion with your child will help you both set the tone for the day. No matter what sort of morning we had, prayer always had a way of bringing us back to a better frame of mind. At times, they need space and grace, other times it's important to be available to talk when they need you.

As my teen became older, I found that nighttime was their favorite time to open up for conversations. For some reason, it was a magic window into their soul. When this happened, I was amazed at the conversations that came up in the late evening. When it happens, I know I needed to be ready to listen.

Lastly, I learned to shut up and listen more. Teens are trying out their ideas, their hairstyles, and their choices. I was terrible at listening and telling my child what to do. I noticed this more and more as he would defer to me during conversations. Part of me recognized that by constantly telling him what to think and what to do, I was crushing his spirit. I needed to let him become the man God intended him to be.

It's also perfectly okay to tell your teen that you don't have it all figured out and that you want their best, too. By demonstrating your authenticity with them, you are creating a space to show them it's okay to not know. They can see in our authenticity that even parents don't have it all figured out, especially with parenting teens. Your relationship with your maturing teenager will change daily. But you can rest in the care and the wisdom that the unchanging Father will guide you through.

Think
How do you continue to grow and develop your role for fostering God's best in your child?

Mindset

CHAPTER THREE

Inspiration and ideas for encouraging your mindset for homeschooling.

"What you heard from me, keep as the pattern of sound teaching, with faith and love in Christ Jesus." 2 Timothy 1:13

Bring What You Have

"Trust in the Lord with all your heart and lean not on your own understanding. In all your ways acknowledge him and he will make your path straight." Proverbs 3:5-6

Bring what you have.

Sometimes what we have doesn't feel good enough in homeschooling. It tends not to be high tech, nor the latest thing and it isn't flashy or cool. Sometimes, bringing what we have means simply showing up. Often showing up is half the battle.

When we bring what we have, we demonstrate we are human, we aren't perfect people, and we don't know everything. At times I show up to the homeschooling day feeling tired, worn out, sad, and discouraged. Other days I show up feeling joyful, inspired, and excited. The critical thing is not how we show up, but *that* we show up and bring what we have.

Throughout the New Testament, Jesus used simple things to share important life lessons. His tools for teaching were ordinary things like bread, wine, fishing, water, wells, grapes, vines, and trees. He taught soul-defining lessons which changed the world forever and lasted centuries upon centuries.

If He could teach revolutionary messages with these simple ideas, we can confidently bring what we have, too.

Instead of seeing what you have as not enough, consider it to be exactly right. When you feel as though your homeschool is lacking, remember Jesus. When you bring what you have, you are sharing in an authentic, life-giving and real way. You are showing that learning isn't about a place; learning is about a way of thinking, a mindset, and can happen anywhere.

Remember your ultimate goal is to encourage your child to have the ability to learn anything. The idea is to show them no subject is too difficult. They have the opportunity to pursue what inspires them, in whatever way they want. There are no limits.

This begins with modelling this idea by bringing what you have. God will find a way to make it exactly perfect in His eyes. He can take what you have and use it, shape it, and mold it into even greater things.

By learning at home, we remove all the distractions of the world in order to put our students in direct contact with wonder. Learning in simple ways is a mindset that will stay with them well beyond the high school years.

Most importantly, we give our kids the gift of time to get to know who they are and how God made them. Our children see the beauty of bringing what they have and through experience, know it's exactly right.

Think
How can you show up today, bringing what you have with joy?

This One Day

"The Lord has done it this very day; let us rejoice today and be glad." Psalm 118:24

I like thinking about homeschooling for only one day.

After the newness of school wears off, I convince myself every day will be hard. With this attitude, every school day feels like working in a salt mine. Voices in my head tell me everyone else's situation is better than mine and everyone else knows what they are doing.

These feelings need to be my reminder to hit pause and take a deep breath. I invite all those fears in, I tell them to sit down, and then let them know they are not in charge. I remind myself to ask the vital questions: "What is needed for *this* day? What do I need to focus on *only for today?*"

God wouldn't lead me down this path only to forsake me when things get hard. As my friend Sarah always says, *"Hard doesn't mean wrong."* As homeschoolers, it's easy to let our fears and insecurities dictate the tone for the day. If you or your child is struggling, it doesn't mean you made the wrong choice.

When things are hard it usually means God is stretching

you to become more in this moment. Even though it feels counterintuitive, struggling is actually a good thing for your family. When we struggle, it reminds us we can't do it in our own strength. It points us back to relying on God to equip us, walk alongside us, and develop our ability to work through difficult things.

This sort of resilience is vital for life. You are together, working side by side in the struggles. Together you are journeying in an environment where you can talk about those things and encourage each other. You are modeling with your child what it looks like to seek God, continue working, and ultimately, persevere.

We don't learn and grow in the easy, successful things. As much as it would be nice to always have it all figured out, to understand all we are learning, and to go about all of our days filled with joy, God doesn't leave us in the safe spaces. He challenges us to learn, grow, and develop tenacity as a result of doing hard things over time.

Ask God to direct your path for this one day. Invite Him in to cover your fears, anxiety, worry, and heavy heart. Remind yourself that this exact experience is how God is shaping you and your family. Let tomorrow worry about itself. Focus only on what you need to do in this one day you have been given.

Think
What is God asking you to focus on only for today?

Elevator Speech

"Let your conversation be always full of grace, seasoned with salt, so that you may know how to answer everyone."
Colossians 4:6

With homeschooling comes a constant: people want to know why you do it.

Be ready to handle this conversation with grace and style. This can be accomplished by having an "elevator speech" – explaining it within the time it takes to ride in an elevator. It needs to be quick, concise, and clear.

In the early days of homeschooling, I was on a mission with my elevator speech. Whenever, people asked me why I homeschooled, I would unleash the fury. I'm sure they were sorry they asked. I poured out every fact, figure, and statistic about how awesome it was. Then I described (with complete arrogance) how superior our studies were to anything they could ever imagine. After all, we were studying Latin. They needed to be impressed and if they weren't, they weren't worth impressing. Did I mention we were studying Latin?

I remember receiving an audit notice from the state in the mail one day and thinking "how dare they question my abilities?" I quickly typed a note saying I was too busy home-schooling to participate in their audit. Then I changed my mind and thought, "Wait, this is my chance to share how incredible we are!" Then I listed every book, every curriculum, every milestone, every test score, and every iota of an achievement. I made sure they knew we were studying Latin, of course. I'm sure they were sorry they even asked.

Later, I had to get real and get over myself. Even if you have a super genius for a student, leading with pride and arrogance won't win any homeschool fans. Believe me, I have met many brilliant homeschool kids, but homeschooling with an egotistical attitude is offensive to everyone.

Usually when people ask why you homeschool, they don't want to know about homeschooling. Actually, they are more interested in proving their assumptions correct. Now whenever anyone asks me, I ask them what they want to know. Then I stop talking.

Let's face it, if they already think homeschooling is a bad idea, chances are you aren't going to change their mind. It's best to set that aside and let it go. If they ever get to meet your kids and see how fantastic they are, that's all they need to know.

Forget about the naysayers. Go create incredible home-schooling ecosystems for your kids. Like a moth to a flame, people will be drawn to the wonder of your curiosity, your vibrancy, and the joy you are designing for your family. Live a homeschooling life so interesting that people have nothing to say except greatness. If people don't get you, they aren't worth getting. These are the people you need to talk to about Latin. Or talk to them about whatever your version is of something that is impressive sounding.

Have an elevator speech ready to tell your story well. While at the same time, live a life so amazing, so fantastic, so incredible, people have nothing but awe and wonder to appreciate. Be bold. Do incredible stuff. This is why you home-school. And, of course, to study Latin.

Think
What will you say when people ask about homeschooling?

It's Not About You

"Remain in me, as I also remain in you. No branch can bear fruit by itself; it must remain in the vine. Neither can you bear fruit unless you remain in me. I am the vine; you are the branches. If you remain in me and I in you, you will bear much fruit; apart from me you can do nothing." John 15:4-5

Homeschooling is hard.

Most people think it is hard because you have to be a super-genius to teach your kid every subject. You don't. They also think it is hard because they think to do it well, you have to become a sacrificial saint like Mother Teresa. This is also not true but having a heart like Mother Teresa would be a gift.

Homeschooling is hard because it's an ecosystem, a mindset, and a way of life. It doesn't start promptly at 9 a.m. and end at 3 p.m., with a bell announcing every hourly change. It is constant. It doesn't go away. It requires dedication, discipline, intention and purpose, day in and day out.

When I get tired, the heaviness of this idea wears on me. All of my child's success or failure is up to me. Whether he gets into a bright, shiny college or becomes a burned-out loser is all on me. If he struggles, my fault. If he doesn't know how to succeed in life, all me. If he isn't good at things that everyone else is a pro at such as calculus, physics, penmanship, cooking dinner, taking care of a home, and doing laundry, I am a failure.

I soon realized this was a pretty small and selfish viewpoint. When things get hard, I know it means that I'm trying to do it in my own strength. When my child struggles, I need to stop. I need to create space for God to work and to give it time. When I think it's all about me, I need to surrender.

Homeschooling should never be all about you. It's about setting a feast of ideas, filled with a table of people who can pour into and bring out the best in your child. You are the preparer and facilitator of the feast. Your child has to do their part and show up, sit at the table, and take in what they are ready for. The nourishing will be at their pace and with the willingness and desire of their passions. Sometimes this learning process is snail-pace slow, and sometimes it's so fast you can't believe it.

This feast of ideas does not rely solely and completely on you. Even if you are teaching every subject to your child, there is a grander work happening. You are nurturing a soul in Christ through homeschooling. You have to do your part and let God do His part. The rest is between God and your child.

Trust that God will guide you, that He will equip you and that He has bigger plans than you can imagine. It requires you to set out the feast for this work to flourish. Surrender the belief and the pressure that everything is all about you. It's not. It's about God and trusting in the plans He has already designed for your family.

Think
How can you surrender the idea that homeschooling is about your efforts alone?

Good Enough

"If anyone will not welcome you or listen to your words, leave that home or town and shake the dust off your feet."
Matthew 10:14

Approval is my Achilles' heel.

I know it's a pride thing. My hope is to care more about what God thinks rather than what the world thinks. In truth, I like for people to think homeschooling is amazing. The reality is, no matter how fantastic your homeschool is, some will still see it as a terrible idea.

It doesn't matter if your student is taking music classes from a Juilliard musician, digging wells in Third World countries, or launching a Kickstarter Starter venture for the cure for cancer. It will never be good enough in some people's eyes. Typically, this comes from the people closest to you and who love you unconditionally. In other words, your family.

Biblically, this makes sense. I think back to the passage in scripture when Jesus goes to minister in his hometown and people criticize him and basically want to kill him. I imagine the people saying, "Who does this Jesus think he is coming here to tell us his wisdom? Isn't he just the son of a carpenter? Let's push him off a cliff."

The people who are supposed to be our best advocates are most often the ones who undermine our hearts the most. Usually, this is not done with a desire to understand. People who know you well typically know how to say things pinpointing your most vulnerable areas. They may ask you questions that sound like:

"Weren't you terrible at math in high school?"
"How could you possibly handle all the hard classes?"
"Won't he miss having friends?"
"How can you be sure you are covering everything?"

They might be right. I might be terrible at math. I might struggle with hard classes. My kid may never have friends in masses like he would at traditional school. I probably won't cover everything he needs to know for life.

However, I can find a lovely math class online. I can enroll him in an equipping community college class in physics. I can create special social activities with other like-minded parents so he and his friends can come together and make memories. I can foster kindness, family, and goodness because I have a voice in his life right now. I can trust God to fill in the gaps.

In the end, you have to accept that your homeschool will never be good enough for some. As Jesus said in Matthew 10:14, *"If anyone will not welcome you or listen to your words, leave that home or town and shake the dust off your feet."* They are seeing as the world sees, not from the place of love.

Forgive and love with grace those that don't understand you. Accept they may never understand you. Focus on the people who love and care for you, unconditionally, and support you no matter what. Those are the ones who matter. Let all of it be good enough in God's eyes.

Think

**How will you handle people who think
homeschooling is a terrible idea?**

Prejudice

"Dear friends, let us love one another, for love comes from God. Everyone who loves has been born of God and knows God." 1 John 4:7

My friend Katie hates sushi.

I still love her even though she doesn't appreciate the beauty of an artfully-crafted rice and seaweed roll. She may be missing out on something good, but I understand sushi is not for her.

Katie's sushi dislike gave me a wise perspective for people who disagree with homeschooling. I don't condemn or think less of Katie for her sushi-loathing ways, I accept it with full understanding. Certainly, everyone has the possibility to homeschool, but not everyone pursues it. Like sushi, home-schooling may not for everyone.

For a long time, I was critical of the traditional school system. It was an easy target when justifying my homeschool actions. With a little research, you find the traditional school-teachers typically spend about four minutes of personalized instruction per student each day.

I clung to this statistic like a cozy blanket. It became my

source of comfort when I first began homeschooling. Certainly, I could do better than four minutes a day. To be sure, for every statistic there is absolutely the other kind of teacher who goes above and beyond for their students. For me it was easier to ignore the above and beyond and only look at the four-minute factoid.

Homeschoolers like me tend to enjoy swapping scary stories about drugs, sex, illicit behavior, and terrible things found in traditional schools. I am guilty of all of these tendencies, along with the notion I am part of some intellectually superior group. I smugly rested in knowing my kid's time isn't wasted on fire drills, active shooter exercises, teacher workdays, assemblies about pop culture topics and pep rallies for sports, which we may or may not care about. I could get really good at mocking those things while puffing up my own ego.

Without saying it out loud, I was fostering the belief that anyone who wasn't homeschooling was not as morally and intellectually elite in my book. I have come to appreciate how wrong, superficial, and prejudiced this thinking is. For every thriving homeschool family, I can think of ten more traditional school families who are thriving in similar ways.

I can appreciate my friend Beth, who homeschooled her children for years, pouring every ounce of herself into it only to find she was exhausted. After putting her students into a solid traditional school, the entire family thrived. Beth could direct her attention to her relationship with her family. It was what her family needed.

I think of my friend Krista, whose family sought refuge in homeschooling for a year after her daughter was bullied in school. The homeschooling year gave her daughter a chance to heal, renew, and refocus. The set-apart season provided the refreshment needed to allow her child to enroll in a school dedicated to the arts, her daughter's true love. Her daughter needed the homeschooling season to grow and rest. Then she could fully thrive in her new school situation, focused on her artistic gifts.

Every family's decision to homeschool or not is intensely personal. Some families choose it for one season and others choose it for their child's entire education. Only God can determine the best path for every individual. There is goodness in all of it. Whether we are on the homeschool journey by choice, by accident, or not at all, it's important to check our hearts. Homeschooling is not for everyone, nor is anyone less of a parent because they don't homeschool. It may be exactly right for my child and my situation. Still, there are plenty of times when sending a child to school out of the home is the most loving thing to do.

We are called to love, first and foremost. Homeschooling is not some secret moral and intellectually elite society. Homeschooling is a choice made out of love, exactly as traditional schooling is a choice made out of love. They both share the same heart for the Father. Allow your attitude about homeschooling to flow from a place of humility.

Think
Where do you see biases in your choice of educational path? How can you surrender this out of love?

Tough Goings

"For I know the plans I have for you," declares the Lord,
"plans to prosper you and not to harm you, plans to give
you hope and a future." Jeremiah 29:11

When things get hard, I want to put on my fix-it hat.

Like most parents, we want our kids to be happy, to do their work with joy, and to be able to understand their academics all the time. We want our days of learning to be effortless, drama free, and fun. When things become difficult, I tend to think everything is terribly wrong.

When challenges come up, I remind myself that some is always better than none. Usually, if we start with some, it motivates us to hang in there and continue to do more. It's the hanging on part that is the hardest. Those days feel like they linger endlessly, and our kids will never get through it.

The hanging in there is what turns out to be the vital lesson. Working through things, sometimes sentence by sentence, word by word, question by question, is precisely where homeschooling gets good. This difficult thing is what will define your kid when they know they can hang on, weather the challenge, and persevere.

My son struggled through chemistry. He had a tough teacher with high demands. He was convinced his teacher hated him and her plan was to destroy his life. Only a slight exaggeration. Frustrated with the weekly work and ready to quit, I came alongside him. We re-read the chapter together. I asked him to explain what he knew, section by section. Some of it he understood, some of it he did not. For the things he did not understand, he looked up more information and then came back to it.

I kept asking him question after question to work through the difficult ideas. Sometimes we took breaks from it and sometimes we had to come back to it over and over again. Bit by bit, we discussed the hard concepts together. Word by word, sentence by sentence, concept by concept and then problem by problem.

I can remember an entire weekend we discussed a particularly difficult idea. What I remember most about walking through that situation was "the look." If you have ever been there when your child began to deeply understand something for the first time, you know what I am talking about. There was the look of relief, almost as if brilliant sunshine washed over his face. "I get it!" he exclaimed.

I share this story not to show how fantastic I am at asking questions. I know nothing about chemistry. I can read and ask him to teach me what he already knows. Where we find gaps in his knowledge, there we can wrestle together. We can look things up and go further. It's in the small, seemingly insignificant places where the magic happens. The wonder is found in the persistent hanging with something, doing the tiny steps over time.

Recently, during a college-admissions visit, the leader asked my son what he was interested in studying. "Chemistry," he said without batting an eye. The look on my face must have been akin to aliens dancing on his head. Will he study chemistry? Maybe. But the idea that he would consider it as a career was stunning. After all he endured, he ended up in a place of appreciation, admiration, and best of all, love.

Little things done well over time build up to an amazing life of learning. Word by word, hard thing by hard thing, and by hanging in there, your family will arrive at amazing places. Beyond learning a subject, the resilience muscles developed in the struggle deliver powerful lessons for life.

Think
How can you stay focused on the little things when homeschooling gets hard?

```
┌─────────────────────────────────────────┐
│                                           │
│                                           │
│                  Worth                     │
│                                           │
│                                           │
└─────────────────────────────────────────┘
```

"For it is by grace you have been saved, through faith—and this is not from yourselves, it is the gift of God— not by works, so that no one can boast." Ephesians 2:8-9

How do you measure your worth in homeschooling?

Is it by test scores, grades, accomplishments, or a smart schedule full of interesting plans? Is it by doing all the things good Christians do like serving, reading your Bible, praying, and going to church? Or is it by going on mission trips, donating your time, money, and resources to others?

For me, it is hard to distinguish my worth in who I am versus the things I do. Because homeschooling feels so ingrained in life, it is hard to separate the two. Who am I in Christ without doing anything at all?

I think if you were to ask me why I homeschooled when I first began, I would tell you it was to get my student into a good college. Since that time, God changed my heart and mind to show me this was a worthy goal, but not the best goal. Ultimately, He convicted my heart to know the real reason I homeschool is about salvation. It's about raising a virtuous young person in Christ.

I don't think I ever set out to make my child my resume or to stock our homeschool full of praiseworthy activity. However, in hindsight maybe I did. If that was the case, it was out of my own insecurities. I told myself I wanted to do it with excellence. But perhaps, I wanted *the world* to think I did it with excellence.

Being academically busy doesn't equate to superior. Test scores aren't my reward or my badge of honor. Having a long list of accomplishments didn't mean I was morally successful. My child was not my trophy. God convicted me that the "stuff" of homeschooling wasn't the point. The stuff of homeschooling was loving Him.

Looking back, I know I made a lot of mistakes. My ego did drive some of the decisions for the things we did, not God. I got a lot of things wrong. Yet my intent ultimately arrived in the right place: to raise a virtuous young man who would love the Lord all the days of his life. Homeschooling worth is not in our accomplishments. My identity is not my child's hopes and dreams.

I think the heart of worth is found in Romans 12:1-2 (MSG), *"So here's what I want you to do, God helping you: Take your everyday, ordinary life -- your sleeping, eating, going-to-work and walking-around life -- and place it before God as an offering."*

That is my prayer. My worth is found in taking all I have, all I do, and surrendering it all, for the love of Him.

Think
How do you define your worth? How can you make all of it an offering for God?

Not Working Ahead

The Lord replied, "My Presence will go with you, and I will give you rest." Exodus 33:14

Long-term planning works really well for things like vacationing in Europe and training for a marathon. Yet sometimes I think God only wants us to focus on what is before us.

There was a time when I tutored an eighth-grade group of homeschoolers in six subjects. Thinking about that now feels pretty remarkable. Not because of my ability to tutor six subjects, but because it was actually fun. I would not have called it fun when I first began, but God taught me valuable wisdom in that season.

In the beginning, I thought of the learning in the traditional school way. I needed to master six subjects. I needed to know everything, work ahead, and be able to explain every aspect of Latin, logic, math, science, English and rhetoric.

This idea worked for about a month, until I was exhausted. I could not master six subjects and do all the other things I needed to do in any given week. I found when I worked too far ahead from where we were in class, I forgot all the details of the material we were focusing on right now. By trying to do it perfectly and in my mind "mastering it," I was my own worst enemy.

Things began to improve when I asked myself, "What do I need to do only for this week?" Instead of feeling as though I had to master it, I thought about what was essential in the week's material. I gave myself grace to not have it all figured out or know every single answer. Sometimes it was much more fun to come to class and say, "Hey, I really struggled with #6 in the math problems this week. Let's work through it together."

It feels counterculture to lead our kids and not have all the answers. In the beginning, I thought it was embarrassing. What I found was on the days when I was least prepared, I was more reliant on the Holy Spirit to show up. I was able to demonstrate grace with myself and model for the kids that sometimes it's even better when you don't have it all figured out.

Without fail, the kids loved to jump in and share their ideas on how to handle the difficult concept. Or, if they weren't sure, they could share what they knew, and we could all collaborate on the idea. Ultimately, we would arrive at figuring it out, feeling better since we grappled with it together and we walked through the steps as a team. For the kids who didn't understand the concept at all, they were able to observe their classmates as a model for the process of how we worked with the difficult concept.

When I was able to relax in the not knowing, I allowed God to show up. This was always better than when I was over-prepared and the master of the subject. I could rest in making space for the kids to struggle and work through things as part of the learning process.

Truly, I think God didn't want me to wear myself out. By encouraging me to focus on this one week, this one day, this one moment, I could rest in Him. He showed me not to work too far ahead and become overwhelmed and exhausted. He invited me to see more of Him by being less of me.

Think
How can you rest in Him? What do you need to do just for today?

The Pause

"Guide me in your truth and teach me, for you are God my Savior, and my hope is in you all day long." Psalm 25:5

When my child asks for help, I'm learning the art of the pause.

This does not come naturally to me. When my son is struggling, my default is to jump in and help out. When he asks my advice for what to write in an email, I want to write it for him. If he needs help with what to say to his boss about his work schedule, I want to tell him. I know this is probably okay for the short term, but this isn't serving him well for the long term.

With homeschooling, it's tempting to want to do things for our kids. Truly, I'm talking to myself here. I find it difficult to let my son struggle in a situation when I know I can help. Plus, he is more than happy to allow me to do it for him. With the pause, I stop to consider: my task or his task?

I can justify my actions all day long. My parents did little to help me navigate the young adult years. I had to figure out every decision on my own. Even though I was completely loved by my parents, I still felt alone in life decisions. I worried constantly about making the right choices with buying a car, applying to college, getting a job and having enough money to pay for everything.

Looking back, it's possible my parents didn't have knowledge in those areas to help me. As a source of pride, I decided early on that my child would never have to figure out everything on their own. I wanted my child to always know they could count on me and I would have their back if they needed it. Yet in hindsight, it may not have been such a bad thing to have to figure life out on my own. My parents might have given me a great gift to know how to do things independently from an early age.

In homeschooling, we have so much ability to design, control, and create our student's ecosystem. It's tempting to extend that same control to the rest of their decisions and the orchestration of their life. I've learned it's important to let them manage and handle as much as they can, as soon as they can.

Yes, we are adults and we are probably better and more experienced at most of the things our kids need to do. It would be faster and easier to get the oil changed in the car for your teen. However, taking them with you and showing them what to do at the oil change station can be part of their life learning. Next time, about 5,000-10,000 miles later, they will know exactly what to do. Learning to let the responsibility rest with them is an important lesson for both parent and child.

Now I'm learning when my son asks for help, I need to pause. Inside my head, I pray for wisdom and not overstepping. Instead of telling him what to do, I ask, "What do you think?" This allows us to have a conversation where the burden stays with him. If he is still stuck, I ask him, "Do you want some coaching on it?"

My hope is to give him space to problem solve out loud on his own before I rush in to save the day. If we end up brainstorming some ideas, it's important I leave the to-dos on his plate, not doing them for him. This is the hardest part. I know it is necessary for him to learn how to problem solve and to own the outcome.

Sometimes the solution is no solution. Sometimes it's resting in the frustration of something that can't be solved. In every situation, the most valuable thing I can convey to my child is that I have every confidence in his ability to figure it out.

Think
When your child brings you a problem, how can you give them the freedom to learn how to solve it on their own?

Seeing More of God

"Everything is possible for one who believes." Mark 9:23

Sometimes I get so caught up in the doing, I forget about God.

I was reminded of this recently by my friend Catherine. In all she does, she carries around an elaborate vision of God. I admire her ability to see situations and people from a greater Kingdom-style awareness. I get so mired in the to-dos, the details, and the drama, I sometimes miss that this is what brings us to God in the first place.

Weekly, I volunteer to tutor middle and elementary school students at my church. Some kids come from difficult situations, some have parents who don't speak English, and some have parents that cannot read or write. The unifying experience is that we love coming together to encourage them all.

Because one of our families was having a difficult time academically, we agreed to meet with the parents and student to discuss how we could come together to support them. I was in "fix it mode" and spent time sharing tools, ideas, and tasks that could be done to move the child's grade up academically. I came out of the meeting feeling a heaviness I couldn't explain. While the parents were grateful and encouraged about the ideas and resources, I felt like I had given them more work to do. It felt flat to me.

Catherine reminded me that this wasn't really about the homework. She reminded me that because we were able to minister to them, to help bring them together, to show them love, grace, and encouragement, it allowed God to work. The family asked about middle school ministry at church and they were able to meet with the pastor.

Part of me felt as though I had been asleep to it all. I came rushing in with my ideas, my to-dos, my agenda, and my fixer-upper plans. Those were all good intentions, but what the family needed was more love, more grace, more healing, more God. The poor academics were a by-product of broken-ness. They needed to see the hands and feet of Jesus.

While I believe homeschooling is an academic endeavor, it reminded me that this undertaking is truly about God. It's about raising virtuous, Jesus-loving children who will follow hard after Him all the days of their lives. Carrie lovingly and gently showed me that I needed to wake up to what this was truly all about. She showed me how to see a bigger God.

As you go about your holy work of homeschooling, remember that while academics, grades, extracurricular activities, and career exploration are important. Take heart that the real reason you are pursuing this is to see more of God. The good stuff is the God stuff. Never lose sight of the fact that all of this is to allow our kids to see a big God at work in their life.

Think

Where are you seeing God at work in your day today? How can you embrace a bigger vision of Him today?

The Perfect Christian Homeschooler

"But seek first his kingdom and his righteousness, and all these things will be given to you as well." Matthew 6:33

God doesn't need us, yet He graciously invites us.

In my mind, being a good Christian meant being completely spent all the time. Extending that to home-schooling equaled exhaustion for Jesus. Unless I was doing, serving, giving, and volunteering all of my time, I wasn't worthy.

In my head, I know that's not true. Yet, when opportunities to volunteer presented themselves, I didn't think twice about saying yes to everything. I didn't pray about it, and I didn't consider my family or my current commitments. It was always yes to everything. My justification was that if God put it in front of me, it was meant for me.

This constant volunteering and serving normally led to my family getting the tired, used-up version of myself when I was with them. I was distracted by the commitments, responding to emails, texts, more work, and more giving of my time. Even when I was with them, I wasn't emotionally with them. The times when I was present, my conversations were filled with complaining about how draining it all was.

Truly, I created some sort of mixed-up version of Christianity. Without intending, I modelled my faith after the Pharisees in the Bible who believed in following a certain set of rules and standards in order to be loved by God. I never said that out loud, but my life was saying it loud and clear.

Who was I when I wasn't serving? Who was I when I wasn't doing things for approval?

As an extension of my efforts, homeschooling became part of this pattern. I began to evaluate whether I was doing things out of love for God or because that's what I imagined perfect Christian homeschoolers do.

I needed to stop. My family deserved more than the tired, burned-out, critical, and judgmental version of me. Clearing away all the distractions of too many activities allowed me to create some breathing room. I wanted to be more available to my family and to Christ.

God didn't need for me to do all these things. I needed to deeply understand I didn't need to earn His love. It was time to let those things go until I prayed over them with purpose and talked to my family about the commitment. It was time to stop saying "yes" to everything and to start letting "no" be a complete sentence.

The time had come to let go of the approval, the legalism, and the judgement. I was ready to live better. If we are Jesus followers, then we know He came so we could have life in abundance. My service and efforts needed to shift to inspiration from a place of wholeness. Jesus didn't come so I could be so busy. He came to give me a life of abundance. This life of abundance included rest, peace, and spaces to breathe.

Think
How are you seeking Him first for direction on commitments in your life?

Cultivating Relationship

"If I have the gift of prophecy and can fathom all mysteries and all knowledge, and if I have a faith that can move mountains, but do not have love, I am nothing." 1 Corinthians 13:2

It's easy to forget about cultivating a thriving relationship with your child in the busy days of homeschooling

My friend Darcy reminded me of this recently. She was right. Operating out of extreme homeschooling mode, every conversation with my child became about schoolwork. In the midst of the chaotic days, I had lost sight of the heart of what mattered.

We both lamented if we are not careful, all of our conversations with our kids can become only about school. She shared that listening to your child is where it needs to start. When everything centers around getting work done, soon our kids will not want to talk to us at all. I know because my child gradually began to shut me out.

I didn't notice it right away. It looked like cutting our conversations short, letting me know he had too much to do. My pressing on him was really about my own anxiety and insecurities. Was he completing what he needed to do? Did he remember to get this or that done? I wasn't asking these things out of care over him as a person. I was asking these questions out of fear.

I know there is a time and a place to check in on schoolwork and how things are going. However, discussing schoolwork all the time with my child was not encouraging. I needed to set clear boundaries with myself on when I would check in on schoolwork and assignments. I needed to resist the temptation to constantly follow up. If my son failed to complete his work, it was on him and his grade would be the consequence.

It was hard for me to make this switch. I had to be intentional about listening and being quiet. My child had become guarded with sharing his personal thoughts around me because he sensed that all I cared about was schoolwork. I had to show him it was safe and okay to be himself by creating a space to let him be.

Developing a better relationship with my son also meant I need to show interest in him beyond school. I had to be willing to learn about things in which I had no interest but knew were important to him. We talked about video games, social media, funny things from the news, sports, and activities he pursued for fun. I focused on keeping it light.

As his social life grew in high school, I aimed to carry a soft touch, not digging too much into personal details or seeking too many facts. My son needed to see it was okay to trust me again with being himself around me, not just his academic self.

I wish I could say we achieved a newfound connection that is deeper than ever. Truly, right now it is a work in progress and sometimes I need to leave him alone. Then there are other times when he opens up for long, fun conversations about neat things that happened from his day.

I know he is still navigating how to be a young adult transitioning from high school to adulthood. I am still learning how to parent a teen who is becoming who he needs to be in Christ. We are both figuring things out and we both need a lot of grace. I'm grateful God continues to work on both of our hearts to allow us to learn this together.

We will never perfect this delicate balance as it is constantly evolving. I'm learning how wonderful it is to be a good listener. I'm learning to let go of being anxious about getting things done. I'm learning to hold things lightly in conversations with my child. Above all, my hope is for my child to deeply know he is loved.

Think
How can you make the relationship with your child the highest priority today?

```
┌─────────────────────────────────────┐
│                                       │
│                                       │
│              Represent                │
│                                       │
│                                       │
└─────────────────────────────────────┘
```

"We are therefore Christ's ambassadors, as though God were making his appeal through us." 2 Corinthians 5:20

We are all ambassadors for Christ. With this same mindset, we have the opportunity to represent homeschoolers, too.

When I tutored a class of eighth graders, I always reminded the students to be good ambassadors for the home-school community. The year involved many field trips, mentor workshops and hands-on activities allowing us to be out and about in our city. People would be making up their minds about homeschoolers based on their actions.

I encouraged them to dress smartly, demonstrate excellent manners, and exhibit Christ-like behavior with integrity at all times. This included the words "please" and "thank you" and leaving things better than we found them by picking up our trash, pushing in chairs, and offering to help clean up the areas we used. This idea of "homeschool ambassadors" sounds like common sense. However, this lesson came about in a difficult way.

At the end of a particularly hard school year, I had taken a middle school team of eighteen homeschool kids to compete in a State Science Olympiad event at a local university. To be honest, I was exhausted and so were the kids. We were sitting through a long ceremony and one of my students was coming unraveled from the emotions of the day. Because I was mentally fried, I had no idea that a little tussle was happening between the student and one of the nearby teams. Picking on an unruly homeschool kid was an easy target. I'm not blaming anyone. Those were simply the circumstances.

The next thing I knew, another team's coach was shouting at me. Her exact words were, "You homeschoolers have no business here in this education competition. If you don't know how to act right, you shouldn't be here. Get your students to behave!"

I pretty much wanted to spontaneously combust or melt into a puddle of tears. I was embarrassed, ashamed, angry, and hurt all at the same time. The behavior of my student was inappropriate, and it was my fault for not keeping it in check. I'm sure we would not earn any points for winning people over to homeschooling that day.

I share that story because it was a reminder to me that people are judging homeschoolers all the time. Whether they are shouting in your face or smiling at you profusely, they are making up their minds about whether or not we are worthwhile people. I'm not expecting to be perfect all the time and we all have our moments. Still, I want people to see homeschoolers in the very best light and with all of the excellence I know so many families demonstrate.

My encouragement is to remind your family to carry that expectation wherever they go. It doesn't matter where they are. They may be helping in the yard, visiting a museum, volunteering in the community, driving down the road, hanging out with their friends, working at a job, or serving in their community. People will be evaluating them and judging them based on the fact that they are Christians first and homeschoolers too. We want to represent not only home-schooling well, but more importantly, Christ.

My hope is that we will give them something joyful and awe-inspiring to consider. It's a good reminder that as we homeschool, people will always be making up their minds and judging regardless. Give them something amazing to see. Show them how light-filled homeschoolers who love the Lord truly are.

Think
How can you represent Christ and the homeschooling community well as you go about your days?

Getting Out of God's Way

"Trust in the Lord and do good; dwell in the land and enjoy safe pasture. Take delight in the Lord, and he will give you the desires of your heart." Psalm 37:3-4

Things don't need to be perfect to be good.

God has been showing me He can still use me even when I don't have it all together. I'm learning to trust Him on that, even if I don't completely get it.

I volunteer weekly at our church, leading an afterschool homework club. On the surface of this group, it's messy, chaotic, disorganized, and clunky. The kids that come are usually maxed out from being at a traditional school all day. The last thing they want to do is sit down and do homework for an hour.

The volunteers who help tutor the kids come for a variety of reasons. Some need volunteer hours for high school, some use it as a diversion from retirement, and others, like me, enjoy pouring into young people. As is true for all humans, they are human. Every day is a surprise potluck of who will show up to tutor and the students to be tutored.

From week to week, despite my best efforts to have it all

organized, it never is. People get sick, have other commitments, Grandma visits, and vacations happen. The reality is on any day I have no idea what tutors or students will show up. To say this drives me crazy is an understatement. I like order and loathe unpredictability. Homework Club is the antithesis of organization.

On one recent Homework Club day, we had the fewest number of tutors and the largest number of students show up. I had to surrender my plans to say, "Okay God, whatever you want."

I had to surrender what I had in mind and let God's plans be what He had for us. His plans are always higher and better than mine. I had to get out of the way. God would use the crazy, lacking circumstances. I had to trust.

By stepping out of the way, I allowed other people to step up. One tutor created a group game that everyone could play, which made for a fun and engaging time for all. Another tutor recruited her husband to come and help, allowing the kids to see what a strong, male, Christian role model looks like. The surrendering and trusting were my chance to let God do what He does best, be God.

I think what God wanted was for me to watch Him work. He wanted the experience for the kids and tutors to be about Him, not about me and my polished performance.

When all of our props, tools, fancy resources, and successes are stripped away, what we have left is ourselves and our Father. I think God wanted the other stuff to stop getting in the way of the true focus for our time.

First and foremost, God wanted to demonstrate the love of the Father with a love for His kids.

Think
How can you keep the heart of your homeschool focused on God?

Mindshifting

"The lions may grow weak and hungry, but those who seek the Lord lack no good thing." Psalm 34:10

"What do you love about winter?" a friend asked me.

For her, winter meant being cozy indoors, reading books, cooking with her slow cooker, wearing comfy sweaters, and hunkering down in chunky blankets. With her question, I found it funny and interesting she assumed I loved winter too.

As a kid growing up in Michigan, I did love winter. Our family would snow ski almost every weekend at a small neighborhood ski area. We took family trips to stay in a ramshackle winter cabin and spent time sledding, skiing, and being together. The cabin did not have running water or an indoor bathroom. Despite the humble appearance, some of my happiest childhood memories are from times spent at that rustic winter cabin.

Winter Sunday afternoons were filled with long stretches of working puzzles or playing board games. My brothers and I would play Life, Monopoly, or Risk for hours on end. In an era before the internet or even cable TV, we always had something fun to do in the winter. At some point as an adult, thinking about winter became associated with the blues or dreariness. Was my happiness in life dependent on the weather?

My friend's funny question about loving winter invited me to shift my mind. Instead of thinking about how difficult winter is, she invited me to view it in a "what's to love" sort of mindset. I find it interesting that when you ask a different question, you begin to see things in a different way.

Bundling up and taking a walk outside in the cold weather is one of my favorite wintertime experiences. My skin feels alive and vibrant from the winter winds and weather. I enjoy noticing how the landscape and wildlife are so different in every season. I treasure how winter tends to bring our family together more often. Without the myriad activities of the spring and summer, we gather as a family to watch a movie or have dinner together more consistently in the winter.

Lastly, I love the dark winter nights when I light candles or have a fire. I appreciate the contemplative nature winter brings. It beckons us to enjoy slowing down and being more in touch with intrinsic aspects of home.

It's easy to let the weather or a negative mindset dictate my moods. As with homeschooling, if the day doesn't go as smoothly as I had hoped, I find it easy to fall into critical thinking. Rethinking my view of winter moved me to think about shifting my thoughts for homeschooling.

As with winter, I can choose to see homeschooling for the goodness it brings. If I'm not careful, I can allow "bad weather" to influence my attitude. Winter can bring a lot of beauty if I look for it. However, to truly see the beauty, I must look deeper than the weather.

Think
Where do you need to shift your thinking?

Disappointment

"Humble yourselves, therefore, under God's mighty hand, that he may lift you up in due time. Cast all your anxiety on him because he cares for you." 1 Peter 5:6-7

My son bombed the SAT this year.

Compared to the prior year, his scores were worse. He sent me a text to woefully report, "Mom, I have gotten dumber." Despite diligently completing test prep and taking dozens of practice tests, he felt his results were an epic failure.

My first reaction was to blame myself. If only I had done more to prepare my child, things would have turned out better. Now he may not even get into any college. I had let him and his future down. It was all on me.

God in His faithfulness reminded me we are more than test scores. With the way only God could, He convicted my heart to remember my child is more than awards and achievements. He was shaping our family in the soul-stretching and emotionally demanding work called life. In His matchless love, He wanted me to surrender the worth I had been placing on my son's standardized percentile rank.

As flawed beings, we can't be in need of a Savior if everything is done without relying on His grace. Sometimes we need to see all of our failures and weaknesses as a chance for the Holy Spirit to show up. Even though we failed miserably, we still raised a virtuous young man who loves the Lord.

Failure is humbling. It requires me to say, "I can't God, but you can." Truly, once you leave high school, does anyone care about what you scored on the SAT? I am learning to keep things in perspective. I reassure myself that God already has in mind the perfect path for my son, even though his test scores are far from perfect.

Resting in God's goodness is so much more satisfying than waving our own. Early on in homeschooling friends said our children would become our greatest teachers. I thought this meant my son would sweetly explain physics or calculus to me over muffins and hot chocolate. I didn't think it would be about seeing my ego, my sins, or my pride on display. Truly, through the homeschooling journey, God allows all of hearts to be refined.

Homeschooling holds up a mirror of ourselves so we can see where God can go to work. Through bombing the SAT and failures like it, we get to practice walking by faith. In these places, God can refine us to be more like Him and to love more like Him. We can even have epic failures in things the world says are important and still be okay. In fact, we are more than okay because God still has us right where He wants us.

Think
How can you trust that disappointment is part of God's plan?

Overcoming
CHAPTER FOUR

Inspiration and ideas for overcoming challenges in the homeschooling days.

"Because he loves me," says the Lord, "I will rescue him; I will protect him, for he acknowledges my name. He will call on me, and I will answer him; I will be with him in trouble, I will deliver him and honor him. With long life I will satisfy him and show him my salvation." Psalm 91: 14-16

Unexpected Light

"Yet you, Lord, are our Father. We are the clay, you are the potter; we are all the work of your hand." Isaiah 64:8

On a spring visit to the North Carolina mountains, a fierce storm kicked up one evening. Thunder and lightning were banging around like an angry visitor. During the dawn of the next morning, I was awakened by glowing dots on the window.

At first, I thought I was dreaming. I got out of bed and pressed my face to the window, sure that it wasn't real. It was. Tiny fireflies were lighting up the forest. Gentle twinkles were blinking throughout the morning dawn. How could this be? Fireflies were things only seen on velvet summer nights, deep into July. Yet here they were, blanketing the springtime woods after an intense storm and sparking their glow despite the circumstances. They were an unexpected light after an oppressive darkness.

That is so like God. Things are hard, oppressive, never changing in our circumstances and we believe it will always be like this. We think the daily grind is constant, nothing new or interesting will ever happen. We march out our days, one after the other without change. We think the storm will never end. Then, fireflies.

In these difficult seasons, I put my head down and stay diligent in the work. Yet in my heart, I am struggling. I want hope. I want something surprising and good. I want new and amazing. I want fireflies every day. But God knows better. He knows only after a time of darkness and struggle can we see His light with clarity.

The secret goodness of our faith is God is always up to something in us. Sometimes we can understand it and other times we have no idea what He's doing. But He is always shaping us, always refining us, and bringing us closer to what He longs for us to be. If we can think of dark times as His loving hands molding us, it feels much better. I want the blessing not the pruning. Yet the pruning is where we learn to appreciate His work.

In some ways, the entire season of high school is one long shaping process. God is molding our family's hearts and minds for what is next in life. Side by side, sometimes independently and sometimes not, we are stewarding our kids into the next season. We are doing our best to prepare them for all that life will require.

With the eyes of loving shaping, we strive to be joyful about hard classes, difficult teachers, critical relatives, challenging disappointments, and failures. In all these tasks and experiences, God is quietly pressing our kids into who they need to become in Him. We never know how these experiences will serve our family in the future.

As I look back through the storms in my own life, I see how they gave me the strength and resolve needed for the next season. God is always at work in us. Through storms, through howling winds, through unexpected light, He is at work in our families every single day.

If we can rest in the promise that God is always up to

something good in us, we can wait with hopeful hearts. We can keep going, keep working hard, keep serving, and keep loving. We can wait for the fireflies.

<u>Think</u>
Where are you seeing unexpected light in your days?

```
┌─────────────────────────────────────┐
│                                      │
│                                      │
│             Fears                    │
│                                      │
│                                      │
└─────────────────────────────────────┘
```

"Do not be anxious about anything, but in every situation, by prayer and petition, with thanksgiving, present your requests to God." Philippians 4:6

My greatest fear in homeschooling is that I'm messing my kid up for life.

I know I am not alone. Many of my friends echoed this same sentiment. There were plenty of days when I felt like this fear was coming true in my family. The days where every challenge reminded me how much easier it would be to send my child to school. The voices in my head saying it shouldn't be this hard and anywhere else would be so much better.

The negative thoughts were a constant through the high school years. I'm confident these fear-laced worries were pretty consistent in most of my friends' hearts too. Having these notions doesn't make you a failure. Having these thoughts is a normal part of the journey. Yet the most important thing is to not let them stop you.

When my child was in a state of laziness, despair, or frustration, my tendency was to react with fear and anxiety, making things worse. When things became hard in homeschooling, I learned that the best response was first to take a deep breath. I needed to slow down, listen, and ask questions. It was critical to go slow, be gentle, listen, encourage and not react. I needed to stay positive and not dive into every fear lurking in my heart.

If I could move past the fear, I could ask the best question: "What is this truly about?" Was my student tired, hungry, anxious, hormonal? Is this a character issue that needs to be addressed? Were there any outside factors influencing their reaction? More often than not, when my child was upset, anxious or freaking out, it was because something else was going on. If I let a little time pass, it would usually work itself out and end up being no big deal. If it continued to be a challenge, there was probably something we needed to work as a team to solve.

Sometimes our kids need to blow off steam. They will do it with the safest person they have, who will love them unconditionally and who has their best interests in mind – you. Typically, when my child would complain or express upset feelings, my response was to whip into problem solving, fix it, helper mode. But almost always, with a little time, things would pass.

Fears are a normal part of the homeschooling journey. Don't let them drive you. Sometimes it's about taking a deep breath. Other times it's about letting your child grapple with the issue and letting some time go by.

More often than not, it's something your child needs to work through in order to develop grit, resilience and tenacity for life. Don't let fear own you. Instead, allow fear to remind you to spend more time with God and ask for His help. If all else fails, a nap, a good snack, and a funny movie are all healing balms for the entire family. Time, prayer, laughter, and His love will see you through.

Think
How will you handle fears in your homeschool?

Stay in Your Lane

"...let us throw off everything that hinders and the sin that so easily entangles. And let us run with perseverance the race marked out for us..." Hebrews 12:1

Keep your eyes on your own work.

Almost every schoolteacher declares this reminder as they pass out a test. It is also helpful advice for walking out the homeschool season. During the high school years, I was constantly tempted to compare my efforts.

Is this class better than that one?

Is this online experience better than what I have?

What are my friends doing?

Are the classes and extracurricular activities good enough for the transcript?

Should my child be volunteering, working or creating a startup company?

Should my child be doing more?

Should I be doing more?

It is so easy to make yourself a constant nervous wreck by gathering information all the time. Certainly, it's important to know what good options are out there. It's wise to understand what opportunities are available for planning the future. However, don't make your homeschool a reflection of your own insecurities.

God has set out a path for you and the only one who can walk this path is you. When we take our eyes off the path God has given us, we are not fully living what He has in mind. We become distracted, insecure, unfocused. Our source of strength needs to be God, not our homeschool.

I love learning about the bright, shiny experiences other classmates are having. When those things rouse my insecurities, I know it's a huge warning sign. What my friends are doing with their homeschooling experiences should not be dictating my plans. The lane God has set out for them is different than mine. I want to walk out my path with confidence. Don't let other's homeschool plans become a source of insecurity.

As the high school years roll on, social things become important. If it makes sense to take an English class with a friend and it's about encouragement and fellowship, by all means pursue it. But do not be afraid to venture down your own path to personalize your child's education, even if it looks different from your best friend's choices.

Keeping your eyes on your own work is vital to operating your homeschool well. Better yet, keeping our eyes on His work and His plans for our homeschool is the best advice of all.

God has given you a race to run. It is a race designed uniquely for your family. Stay in your lane and run it well.

Think
How can you stay focused on the path God has designed for you?

Stay Curious

"Brothers and sisters, I do not consider myself yet to have taken hold of it. But one thing I do: Forgetting what is behind and straining toward what is ahead." Philippians 3:13

My goal is to not "smother mother" this school season.

I long for my son to do things for himself, manage his schedule maturely, and step up. Yet, when I see him struggling, I swoop back in to micromanage the process. When I overexert myself into his life, I undermine his abilities by constantly smoothing out this process.

Somehow, I equated his failure meant my failure. Truly, everyone fails, everyone makes mistakes. It's through these mistakes we grow and learn. To try to create a mistake-free life is impossible.

I see my son struggling in his history class and trying to manage a new and hefty workload. My first temptation is swoop in, organize it, and help him map out the workload.

This time I've decided to take the approach suggested by a good friend. She said, instead of being the "task master," be the "question asker." She said, "If you stay curious with them, it helps them think through how to manage a situation well. Ultimately, if they own it, the outcome will be better no matter what."

My mindset switched from "Do it this way" to "What do you think is the best way to do this for you?" Instead of telling him all the ways he can manage his workload, I invited him to come up with ways to manage it for his style.

I must do my part by peeling my fingers away. I have to give him space to work his plan and fail, if needed. I have to be busy with my own life and let him know I trust him with his. Ultimately, when I swoop back in it says, "You can't possibly do this on your own; let me do it for you." It's a vote of no confidence.

By staying curious, it's walking alongside him down the road and allowing him to navigate it. It's not shouting at him from way down the path saying, "Get here!" or "Go this way!" It's letting him find his feet for his adult life. It's allowing him to see the journey from his own experience of discovery.

I believe this is the hoped-for vision of parenting well: inviting our kids to learn how to navigate their own way. It's about encouraging them to listen to God's voice for how to walk out their own life. This is how they become confident in their faith and know with certainty the way to the Master.

Think
How can you stay curious when your student struggles?

Persevering

"Let us not become weary in doing good, for at the proper time we will reap a harvest if we do not give up." Galatians 6:9

My son wanted to quit.

He spent months trudging through a Microeconomics class, which seemed like a good idea back in the sweet days of summer. Now, at the end of the first semester, he had a solid D.

As a parent, I was trying not to freak out. I didn't want the "what if" thoughts to cloud my mind. What if this one class destroys his GPA? What if this class wrecks his chances of getting into any college? What if this hurts his ability to quality for scholarships? I was trying not to allow fear to be the boss of me.

My son had seen other students struggle with hard classes and then drop them. He also knew about the option to move the class to a no grade "audit" status. He was pushing hard for us to let him off the hook. I understand there is a time to cut your losses and drop a class if your family is going through a tough season. However, my husband and I felt this was an opportunity for our son to develop grit and persevere.

I wanted to quit, too. I didn't like being in this position of having so much riding on this class. We decided to stay with it and come alongside him. We didn't take over, but we did discuss strategies on how to work through the materials. A few times, we read through a chapter together and discussed it. On long car rides, we had conversations to think through some of the concepts in a deeper way.

Through hard work, my son slowly, and steadily, improved his grades. We were not geniuses in the subject matter to offer help, but we did what we could. We discussed the chapter with him and asked questions. We asked him to explain things in his own words. It wasn't fancy and it didn't require a tutor or someone with a master's degree in the subject. What it did require was my son's attention, focus, and time to work through the material. In this situation, my son needed someone to come alongside him in the most literal sense. We didn't have a lot of knowledge, but we offered our presence and coaching in a hard situation.

The takeaway from the struggle was rich. Along with sticking with something difficult, my son learned many life lessons. He learned to advocate for himself in the class by asking for help. He also asked the instructor if he could go back through his tests for half credit on the questions he missed. The instructor was gracious in allowing him to rework the material. When looking back over the coursework from the beginning of the year, my son shared, "I don't know why I made this so hard. It's actually really easy once you understand it."

Maybe my son needed time and space to marinate on the subject. Perhaps his brain wasn't oriented towards a passion for Microeconomics. Even so, he learned that perseverance, even when it's hard, can be rewarding. He learned sometimes things take longer to understand. With time, effort, and dedication, he would eventually arrive at a place of understanding, if he hung in there. He learned people will give you grace and extra credit, sometimes, if you ask for it. Or not. But if you ask with kindness, chances are you will get it.

Even though the class did not end up being a top grade, it taught my son and our family so much. I'm grateful my son had the experience of walking through a difficult situation while he was still at home. I'm glad we were able to come alongside him to encourage him and remind him to be persistent.

It's tempting to want to shield our kids from hard things. However, by encouraging them to stay the course and trust in the Lord, they develop strength and tenacity they need for life.

Think
How can you encourage your child to stick with it when they face hard things?

The Alien Who Sleeps Upstairs

"We love because he first loved us." 1 John 4:19

I simply asked my son to pick up his towel.

Before slamming his bedroom door, he lobbed the missile, "I can never do anything right!"

I didn't think the phrase, "Please hang up your towel" would create a nuclear meltdown. Apparently, I was wrong.

At times, my teenager can take my requests with a no-big-deal attitude as if to say, "Oh, of course. Why didn't I think of that?" At other times his response feels like, "I know you have secretly hated me all of my life." I know he has a lot of stuff swirling in his brain: college applications, girls, fitting in, friends, applying for jobs, learning how to drive, classes, and what to do after high school. I know it's a lot.

I struggle with whether to let it be. In the grand scheme of things, is towel hanging critical? Does it truly matter if he hangs up his towel? With wisdom, he will understand having a towel on the floor means it doesn't dry properly. Towels on the ground pick up whatever creepy crawlers might enjoy staying there. Ultimately, the towel on the floor will become the teacher for him without me saying a word. I still don't have to like it. I want my kid to be a functioning part of the world. I want him to see the subtleties of life and realize things are much better if you hang up your towel.

I think something deeper is at work here. My son is tired of my nagging. He knows soon he will not have to be subjected to my constant evaluation of his efforts. I perceive my comments as helpful hints for how to live best. To him, it feels like a constant deluge of Improvement 101. He wants to be treated like a grown up; I want him to act like one.

The teenage years can feel emotional and endlessly drama-laden. I'm praying for wisdom to know what my son needs most from me. Even though he's not gone yet, I miss my son. He's already gone in so many ways. I miss the days when conversations were easy and sarcasm wasn't the underlying tone of the day. Every so often I catch glimpses of the son I remember and I am reminded he is still there.

I trust in the fact that this is only one season. In a year or so from now, I know it will change yet again. I hope and pray for my son to see God at work in his life. I pray my child can hear His voice as mine is being shushed. I have to trust that all will be well in God's plans for him. Even if he doesn't hang up his towel.

Think
How can you love your child when they act unlovable?

Sick Days

"Peace I leave with you; my peace I give you. I do not give to you as the world gives. Do not let your hearts be troubled and do not be afraid." John 14:27

As a parent, part of me secretly loved sick days.

Not serious illnesses -- I'm talking simple colds and sniffles. No one would ever wish for their child to be sick. For me, having the chance to give my teenager some TLC and him actually appreciating it, was a nice feeling. Without having to be productive in any way, a sick day feels like a grace day from school.

That is until I try to make the sick day productive. I'm ashamed to say sometimes I did try to get my sick child to do schoolwork. Even though he clearly wasn't well, I convinced him that he could certainly read or watch an educational video.

My son would be running a fever and sucking on ice chips and I would be handing him a book to read. Some weird derangement would kick into my brain with voices saying, "You're going to get behind. Everyone else is already far ahead in this class. You're going to fall so far behind that you will never catch up." Those fearful voices can make you do ridiculous things, like trying to get your child to do work when they clearly feel terrible.

Don't be like me. When your child is sick, let them be sick and call it a grace day. Give yourself rest to believe it will be just fine. As parents, we know the difference between when our kids are truly sick, or simply not up to the task. Try not to let fear consume you and overthink it.

Sometimes our kids need a mental break. This is where your detective skills come into play as a parent. Are they really sick or do they need a day to reset and recover? If sick days become a habit, you may need to look deeper.

My sister and her daughter used to sometimes celebrate "fake sick days." Those were the days when everyone needed a personal reset. They would rest, take naps, and watch movies all day. They weren't truly sick, but both needed a day of renewal together. I'm not suggesting you take a fake sick day, but there may be a day when you both need some fun and rejuvenation.

When sick days come, let them be days to rest and recover. Don't try to be productive unless your child wants to do something in their bed. It's perfectly okay not to be productive or feeling well all the time. This is part of the homeschooling journey. Plan that things will not go as planned sometimes.

Most of the world thinks homeschoolers stay in their pajamas and read in bed all day anyway. Consider this your way of contributing to the world's vision of homeschooling when you need it. Trust that it's going to be okay. Have a cup of tea, pray, and rest. Let it be a day of recovery for everyone.

Think
When things don't go as planned or your child is sick, how can you rest, too?

```
┌─────────────────────────────────────────┐
│                                           │
│                                           │
│            Be Here Now                    │
│                                           │
│                                           │
└─────────────────────────────────────────┘
```

"Therefore, we do not lose heart. Though outwardly we are wasting away, yet inwardly we are being renewed day by day." 2 Corinthians 4:16

It's been raining for a week straight. A tropical island escape sounds like a good idea right now. I want to be anywhere other than where I am, facing this season.

I know it's normal to have blue days. Everyone has those kinds of weeks where your car is in the shop with an expensive repair, your family is sick, a friend cancels on a commitment she made to help you, the house is dirty, and the dog smells like a dog. Your homeschooling feels unproductive and as if it will never end.

When I am able to get some perspective, I realize this is called "life." I want to wish it away and fast forward to sunshine days. I desire the kind of day when your kid reads a book and suddenly has a brilliant insight which amazes you. The kind of day you get a card from a friend telling you how much your friendship means. Top it all off with your husband surprising you with flowers, even though it's not your birthday or anniversary.

These hum drum, ordinary gray days are also vital. These nothing special times remind us how treasured the good days are. How can I see difficult days with beauty? How can I change my mind to find gratitude for days that don't appear lovely on the surface?

It's okay to acknowledge homeschooling is hard at times. I'm working on accepting what God has given me in this moment. It's okay to feel annoyed, to be upset, and to not love homeschooling or even like it sometimes. Nothing is always sunshine and roses.

When I feel this way, I think slowing myself down is helpful. When I take time to write down my thoughts, clear my head with exercise and giving myself kind self-care, I come to a place of peace. Drinking lots of green tea, watching funny movies, and listening to encouraging sermons helps me shift my mind from the difficulties and onto something better.

Wishing these things away or thinking the good life is way off in the distance isn't serving anyone. This is my life now. The ordinary, difficult days are also part of the good life. How can I find beauty in them?

Yesterday I left a shop and was walking in the rain. At first, I was unhappy about being wet. Looking at a barren tree, dripping with rain drops, I was inspired to recognize they looked like tiny crystals. The tree, in its dormant season, is drawing nutrients, strength, and energy for a season soon bursting with leaves and flowers. Even though the tree was mostly bare, it was still beautifully covered with the crystal raindrops.

My hope was to be like the tree, drawing in beauty and goodness as I prepare for the season ahead. Beauty is here now, if I have eyes to see it.

Think
What encourages you when things get hard?

Comparison

---

*"Let the peace of Christ rule in your hearts, since as
members of one body you were called to peace. And be
thankful. Let the message of Christ dwell among you richly
as you teach and admonish one another with all
wisdom through psalms, hymns, and songs from the Spirit,
singing to God with gratitude in your hearts. And whatever
you do, whether in word or deed, do it all in the name of
the Lord Jesus, giving thanks to God the Father through
him." Colossians 3:15-17*

My ego is embarrassing at times.

I recently sat with a friend who talked nonchalantly about her son's high-achieving academic status. She shared stories clearly demonstrating his ability to do hard things, working diligently at his job, school and faith. He was doing all the right things with discipline, excellence, and goodness.

Instead of celebrating how her son's efforts glorified God, I was quietly dying inside. She talked about him in a loving way that wasn't bragging, but simply a matter of facts. My face was smiling and I was heartily cheering for her and her son, on the outside. But inside I felt jealous, discouraged, and angry. And I was ashamed of myself.

How was it that her family's victories equated to my life being less? The next morning, I spent time on my knees in prayer, crying out to God. I asked for forgiveness for my jealous and comparing heart, and I asked for God to help me find a better way to think about all of this. I needed to lay it down. I needed to surrender my ego and my comparison heart.

Why couldn't I feel joy on the inside for my friend? I love my friend and I love her son. I long to be glad for them, not only on the inside, but with my whole body. Why was it that all these things became about me and my own ego?

I know I serve a big God. I know He has designed a race for each of us to run. I have to trust that even though my son's race may look different, it is the one God has placed before him. Even though certain aspects of life don't come easily for my child, he has gifts God has bestowed upon him. God didn't declare certain gifts better or higher than others. They are all God's perfect gifts for how He made us.

Somewhere in my mind, I decided my friend's joys meant I was a failure. I had made the situation about myself and my ability to create a world-worthy outcome. Knowing someone else who is better, smarter, and more successful than our family exposed my sin-filled nature.

There will always be people who are smarter, better, and more successful than me or my family. My eyes need to be directed to God for His approval. I needed to let go of what the world deems a success. I can only run my race in the best way I know how, with excellence, prayer, dedication, and goodness. The rest is up to God and my son. I encourage the road and the resources, but the race is his to run.

God is not limited in His abilities to bestow good gifts. Even though my child's gifts may not look like everyone else's, they come from a God who loves us. His love isn't about our achievements or our successes, but for who we are in Him.

Think
How do you handle comparison? What do you need to surrender in order to take up God's vision for your child?

"The Lord himself goes before you and will be with you; he will never leave you nor forsake you. Do not be afraid; do not be discouraged." Deuteronomy 31:8

Have you ever had a feeling of disappointment you can't explain?

For me, it feels like an anxiousness resting just below the surface. The telltale signs are when I am endlessly procrastinating and feeling aimless. As I scroll through social media, email, and websites, I search for something to make me feel better. Even though I desperately try, I never find it.

Maybe this new fitness routine or this shiny new book, or perhaps this curriculum will work better. There must be something to help me feel happier, more content, and more peaceful. It could be fresh new outfit or a snappy pair of shoes to perk me up.

In truth, I need more of God.

Even though I know the world will always disappoint, I often need to be reminded that nothing will ever satisfy like God. I could be doing all of the right things -- praying, reading the Bible, talking to friends, praying some more. And yet, there can be days when life casts a grayness over my soul that I can't shake.

What's going on here? What is wrong?

When I find myself in a funk, I know I need to do some reflecting to figure out what is underneath all of this. I like to journal, getting things out of my head and onto some paper. Others might need to talk about it, pray about it, or fast about it. For me, I turned to pen and paper and wrote the words down, "What is wrong here, really?"

I started the page with "Dear Lord…" and then I proceeded to write down all the big and little things that were bothering me. Big things on my heart were questions like, "God, what is my true purpose?" or, "God I don't feel like I'm enough." Little things nagged at me, too. I wrote those thoughts down asking God, "Why can't I have more fun?" or "Why do I feel so unproductive?" I poured out to God in desperation asking why all of life was so hard and why I wasn't getting any answers from Him. I asked God to help me to embrace this season. I was ashamed and embarrassed that I was struggling so much when as a Christian, I have every reason to live with joy, purpose, and goodness. What was wrong with me?

God in His goodness helped me see my expectations were what was taking me down. My wrong expectations or worn-out ideas were silently killing me. Expectations that every day would be productive, every day I would feel happy or that there wouldn't be days of battle and struggle. Changing my expectations helped me gain perspective. In some cases, this meant releasing the expectation or perhaps having no expectation at all.

When I could find a way to surrender my strict plans for myself and my life, I found it was easier to laugh, to be in the moment, and to be open to new things without the guilt of achievement. I could see more of the very things I longed for.

I had to give it all to God and invite Him to help me see things differently.

Expectations can be helpful, but they were harming me more than they were serving me. Lately, I have changed my "expectations" to "intentions." As I plan out my week, I jot down my intentions for what this week might look like and how it might serve the Lord, and my family. The word "intention" holds a lightness that fits me. It casts a warmth of goodness. There is a sense of freedom in it. In Christ, we were meant to be free. By releasing the expectations, I could embrace the extravagant freedom in Christ.

Think
What are your intentions this week? How can you hold them with a lightness?

```
┌─────────────────────────────────────┐
│                                     │
│                                     │
│              Seasons                │
│                                     │
│                                     │
└─────────────────────────────────────┘
```

"May the God of hope fill you with all joy and peace as you trust in him, so that you may overflow with hope by the power of the Holy Spirit." Romans 15:13

It's been a rough season.

This has been a season of broken collarbones, ailing family members, funerals, health scares, and in the midst of it, homeschooling. How do you stay diligent when all you want to do is go back to bed?

I'm not sure I have all the answers, but I do have one answer -- God. I've been pressing into Christ like crazy this month, asking Him for the provision I need, the wisdom I need, the energy I need. I ask Him for the daily portion for this one day.

When I feel depleted by life, it is easy for me to want to skip the time spent in the Bible and in prayer. I have to remind myself to do it anyway. Sometimes it's one passage, one sentence, one page. My aim is to stay rooted in the Word as though my life depends on it. This month, I have been carrying a piece of scripture in my pocket and pulling it out often. Do whatever you need to in order for the Word to provide you with encouragement.

When I'm struggling, I know I need to be my own best mother. This means doing all the things I know how to do to take good care of myself. As the world crumbles around me, the last thing I want to do is eat right, exercise, and rest. But that is always exactly what I need. Be your own loving mom. Sitting outside in the sun, taking a walk to the end of the street, drinking a glass of water, taking a nap. Any little thing I do to offer myself healthy nurturing, I do it with love and intention.

In these intense seasons, I have to remind myself to stop the madness. It's easy to slip into "ninja worrier" mode (not ninja warrior.) I encourage myself to focus on the now. I notice my breathing and devote my full attention to the task. I pray like God is right next to me all day as my constant companion. I focus on gratitude.

When hard seasons come, I know this season is only a season. At times, we needed to set schoolwork aside to manage a crisis. Sometimes we only listened to an audiobook or completed school in the car. Sometimes the whole school day was chucked and we headed to a park for a reset. I know there will be brighter days ahead and I cling to the promise that God is always faithful in His care of my family.

When the burden is too much for me to carry on my own, He will. Still, it requires that I first surrender it to Him. I must rest, pray, trust, and ask for one daily portion from Him. Deeply, I know these types of moments are exactly why we homeschool. It is through weathering the storm together as a family, trusting in our God, and staying diligent in the days that we grow deeper in Him. I have to remember, that there is still learning happening. We are learning that no matter how hard life gets, we have a Savior who can overcome anything.

<u>Think</u>
How can you press into Christ through hard seasons?

The Authenticity of Winter

"I go to nature to rest my eyes. I go to nature to connect with something broader than I can understand." -- Notes on Nature Journaling, Claire Walker Leslie

Wintertime is the season when plants do their most important work. They are storing energy, deepening roots, and preparing for the growing season ahead. When you think about the wintertime homeschooling season, we are exactly like the plants. We are inward focused and carefully storing away knowledge in preparation for the coming days.

I like the authenticity of this idea. I like that we are readying our hearts and minds for a season of bursting forth in showy wonder. Despite the quiet appearances, we are stowing away good conversations, excellent books, and daily sustained efforts. Truly, not every day is about goodness, but hopefully, most days are marked with a nice rhythm of purposeful efforts.

This season I picked up a little hobby of nature journaling. I started creating a nature journal with my son as a science-style effort to practice observational skills. He quickly dropped out of our nature journaling times, but I continued.

I loved how it forced me to be in the moment, to concentrate deeply on beauty in my midst. I could do it terribly and still find a sacred place to explore my own interests. With my son launching from home in a few years, my desire is to cultivate habits for life beyond homeschooling.

Let's face it, if we are doing our job as homeschoolers, we are creating learners who are curious for life. The best way to do that is to model for our kids that we, too, have passions beyond homeschooling.

This past week I bundled up and sat outside in our recent snowfall to take in my surroundings. At first, I thought how quiet everything was. However, the more I listened, the more I heard. What started as silence, transformed into vast and elaborate symphony of songs from a variety of birds. There was so much happening, but I had not been still long enough to notice it.

I wonder if God thinks about our lives like that. We think everything is the same and nothing is changing and all the while, God is busy designing so much wonder for our lives. He can't wait to reveal it to us when we are ready. I'm reminded of this promise from Isaiah 43:19:

> "See, I am doing a new thing!
> Now it springs up; do you not perceive it?
> I am making a way in the wilderness
> and streams in the wasteland."

From the world's perspective I sometimes forget that idea. On dreary days, I can get lost in the drudgery and the ordered homeschool steps that feel like a never-ending trek. Friends share stories from their shiny brick school, glossy technology projects, and exciting plans for the rest of their year. I feel ordinary in my winter season of preparation.

Winter strips away everything. The idea of winter is not necessarily confined to the cold months, either. Wintertime seasons can be any time of the year. Authentic seasons are the ones that bring everything back to the elemental form in order to prepare for the season ahead. It can be a hard season, but we can keep our hearts and minds fixed upon the hope of all that God is preparing to send our way. I can sit in a snowstorm and discover fresh beauty. I can remember days of wonder from years past. I can treasure it all.

I can look to the future with anticipation by keeping my heart focused on God's coming promises. Just as with the bird songs that I did not hear at first, all of God's goodness will be revealed when we are ready for it.

Think
How can you stay faithful in the ordinary to see more of God's extraordinary?

Letting the Difficulties
Transform You

*"Not only so, but we also glory in our sufferings, because
we know that suffering produces
perseverance; perseverance, character; and character,
hope." Romans 5:3-4*

People always say that deep hardships bring deep blessings.

It's hard to hear those words in the midst of the difficulty. I desire the transformation of the hardship without all the pain. I realize this probably sounds childish and shallow. I want the fruit, not the difficulty.

When my child complains about how hard something is or how he will never understand hard math, I want to make it easier. The homeschooling journey has taught me that sometimes trying to make things easier truly makes things worse.

Not releasing my child to figure things out is actually doing them a disservice. Those are the moments when I wish someone would have gently tapped me on the shoulder and said, "Step away from the snowplow, Mama."

In case you don't know what a "snowplow parent" is, they are the ones who at the first sign of trouble, get out the proverbial snowplow. Snowplow parents remove obstacles for their children, so they never have to struggle with difficulties. I tend to justify my actions like with phrases like, "Just this one time" or "If I help in this small area, then he can take it from there." I am only fooling myself.

I end up doing too much and my child resents it. They assume my helping is because of my lack of faith in their abilities. Then my child shuts down and decides he will not share struggles with me in the future. The difficulties are there to help both of us to strengthen our struggle and tenacity muscles. My son needs to learn perseverance. I need to learn how to listen, encourage and step away from the problem that is not mine to fix.

I'm better at it now. It doesn't happen perfectly every time, but I'm slowly learning how to move away from the snowplow. Instead of jumping in to help, my first step is to empathize using words like, "Wow, that must be frustrating" or "I can imagine that must feel pretty difficult for you right now." Next, I ask clarifying questions such as, "Are you looking for ideas or do you only need to vent?" Or perhaps, "Do you want some coaching on it or do you just want me to hear about your struggles?"

When my student is stuck, most often he just wants someone to hear him and see him in the midst of it. He wants a loving encourager to acknowledge that this is challenging work. Usually, my son does not want my solutions. He already knows what to do. He needs someone to see him in the midst of it all and say, "I see you and I love you. Keep going." Rarely does he want help with problem solving or ideas. He only wants me to see him in the midst of his situation.

I didn't understand this until way too late in our homeschooling journey. As a parent and teacher, it's hard to separate loving your student from the notion that sometimes what they need is time and space to work it out. In those moments, we can remind them how much they are loved by God and by us. We can remind them we have confidence in them. Giving them room to figure it out might be the most loving thing we can do. Those difficulties are the transformative work that strengthens parents and students as a result. Trust God to allow the hard things to transform you and your child.

Think
How can you allow space for your God and your child to work out difficulties?

Laying Down Perfection

*"As for God, his way is perfect: The Lord's word is flawless;
he shields all who take refuge in him." Psalm 18:30*

If no one lives a life of perfection except Jesus, why do I
expect it in my life?

Scrolling through social media, it feels as if everyone's life
looks so much glossier than mine. Posts of an amazing family
vacation, students winning awards, everyone beautifully
dressed up for a celebration, and shares of the sweet things
their child did that day. Everyone else's kids are perfect and
everyone's lives are so much more fun than mine. This was the
lie I was telling myself and I chose to believe it.

In this particular moment, my child was snapping at me
about his chores. He was struggling to manage life, balancing
a job, the pressures of academics, and figuring out what
to study for college and career choices. This was not a highlight reel moment to be shared on my social media feed. Will I
survive this season? Will my child ever get through these
years?

Yes. And yes.

I needed to remind myself social media is not reality. It was making me feel terrible and I needed to stop looking at it. In a moment of clarity, I decided to take a break and took it off my phone. I decided to use the same time for something better with praying, reading the Bible, taking a deep breath, sitting in the sunshine, or drinking a cup of tea. It will all still be there for me if I decide to return to it. Or maybe I'll finally realize there is a vibrant life to be lived outside of my screens.

Reading the statistics about how much time people spend looking at social media in a lifetime, I found that it adds up to more than a year of life. An entire year spent reading about other people and their posts. I decided I wanted better than that.

Social media distorts our views of what is reality by looking at life through the lens of curated, beautiful moments. No one ever posts pictures of their child's worst moments or their greatest personal struggles. Life isn't perfect. Somehow, I thought it needed to be in order to be happy.

Perfectionism was an area I knew God wanted me to prune and in which He wanted me to mature. I decided God was using these feelings to cause me to lean into Him. Quite possibly He wanted to use this struggle for good things that are coming next. I needed to be awake to the growth opportunity by letting go of the perfection mindset. Social media wasn't serving me well. I needed to choose higher and wiser.

If I kept holding on to perfection as my sense of measurement, I would never enjoy anything. Nothing would be good enough. If I were to wait until my life was organized, lovely, peaceful, and streamlined, I would never do anything. For me, learning to embrace things in their full imperfection made them true and authentic. I needed to change my mind. Things don't have to be social-media-worthy on the outside to be worthy in my heart.

The true, good, and lovely things in our lives usually come from messy, chaotic, and unbeautiful places.

<u>Think</u>
How do you give yourself and your family grace while longing for perfection in Christ?

Change Your Mind

"And let us consider how we may spur one another on toward love and good deeds." Hebrews 10:24

Have you ever experienced "stinking thinking?" I'm ashamed to say I was recently doing exactly that and of all places, in church.

On Sunday morning while I was supposed to be worshipping, I was thinking terrible thoughts about family, my husband, my child, myself and probably my dog. Church is usually the one place I can count on to activate my personal reset. I can close my eyes and cover my family in prayers of renewal and remembrance of the Jesus I desperately need. Why was I having such a hard time letting go of my stinking thinking?

I asked God to change my mind. I confessed all my stinking thinking thoughts. I felt humbled and unworthy and weak in all the areas where I should feel strong. After all the years I've spent in church, in small groups, in women's fellowship and serving, in reading my Bible, and in praying, I thought I would be more enlightened by now. Why wasn't I further along in living out my faith? Why was it such a struggle for me to be present in this day of Sabbath? Why did I feel like such a failure in my heart?

God whispered to me, "I still love you."

What's amazing about our faith in God is nothing can ever separate us from His matchless love. No matter how many terrible, passive aggressive thoughts we have, no matter how many times we say things we regret, no matter how many stinking thinking thoughts we have, our God still loves us.

The message during service that day was about why we go to church. At first, I thought how simple and obvious it is to attend church. It's the Lord's Day, it's what Christians do, it's to profess our faith and practice our commitment. But the pastor reminded us that being in church is more than that.

Attending church on Sundays is about each other. We gather on Sundays to be reminded of our faith and to practice worship, absolutely. But more importantly, as scripture says, we attend church to "spur one another on." Hebrews 10:24 says, *"And let us consider how we may spur one another on toward love and good deeds."*

Being in church reminded me it's about encouraging each other. I desperately needed spurring on that day. I needed to be reminded by the body of Christ. I needed to physically separate myself from my selfish thoughts and rest in the community of believers. I needed to see other Christ followers, with smiles and tears and hugs and laughs and illness and new babies. I needed to be reminded we are all here not only for ourselves, but one another. We are all part of learning to live out our faith together.

I have come to view Sunday mornings as not only showing up for God and experiencing His great power. Sundays are also about showing up for each other and moving past our own smallness of thoughts and fears. That Sunday morning, I started off in a place of darkness, sadness, and failure. But God, as He does so faithfully, reminded me in all these things we are not alone. We are so loved.

Like Sunday mornings, homeschooling gives us the opportunity to keep showing up no matter the status of heart. When we show up, we allow God to do His thing. Then, equipped with His great love, we can pour out this offering.

<u>Think</u>
How can you keep showing up for God? How can you be reminded of His great love?

Yet the Lord longs to be gracious to you; therefore he will rise up to show you compassion. For the Lord is a God of justice. Blessed are all who wait for him! Isaiah 30:18

"I don't get Jesus," my teenage son recently said to me over breakfast.

Trying not to have a crazy reaction, I calmly asked what he meant. He went on to explain that he didn't get the relationship he is supposed to have with Jesus. He was confused by the Holy Spirit everyone talks about, the feeling that Jesus is real. He was full of doubts.

As a family, I thought we were so far past this place. Hadn't I done all the right Jesus things? We had devotions each morning, we prayed, we read the Bible, we attended church, and he was surrounded by Christian friends. Hadn't I checked all the "guaranteed Christian child" boxes? And yet here he was full of doubts.

Maybe I was a fraud to him. Perhaps he looked at our family representation of faith and then wondered how in the world this could be true. Was I not walking out my faith? Was

I really a surface Christian simply doing all the right things? Could it be he saw through our thin faith?

I thought I had done so many things right. Yet somehow, I missed the vital and essential piece of helping him get his relationship with Jesus right. I felt as if I had failed my son. I failed on perhaps the most important thing, the only thing that really matters.

In that moment, I wish something brilliant had come to me to convince my son about how life-giving and forever changing his relationship with Jesus could be. I wish I had thought to talk about my own doubts in faith and that it is a journey. But I didn't. I sat there dumbfounded and without hardly anything to say other than, "How about praying about it and asking Jesus to show you?"

When I thought about my own faith walk, it wasn't found in the doing. It was found in the waiting. It was in the times that I fiercely struggled, pressed into my own doubts, and found Him there. Sometimes the bravest thing you can do is wait.

I think of my friend, Kristine, with cancer -- plodding through treatment after treatment, waiting for healing, waiting to get her white blood cell count to go down, waiting to know if the cancer is growing.

I think of my brother, struggling with an unknown, soul-debilitating ailment that could be a simple thing or a rare form of aggressive disease. He waits for answers that may never come. Not knowing may be the only answer.

I think of my son who sits in doubt of his faith. He searches for answers and he dismisses most of them. I pray every day for him that Jesus will pierce his heart. I pray Christ will give him a glimpse of this beautiful, life-giving relationship that will cause him to follow hard after Him all the days of his life.

I know my child's faith has to be his own. I understand and appreciate that our kids must walk their own path to

Jesus. But I don't want to accept it. I understand it's by wrestling with his own faith that my son will discover his relationship with Jesus. Or not. It is not up to me, it is between my heavenly Father and my son.

For now, I wait. My prayers flow with a desperation like never before. I sit at the feet of Jesus and plead for him to reveal Himself to my son. I surrender my son to Him knowing our children are only ours for a little while. I tearfully and achingly place this humble prayer in my Father's hands. I remember that sometimes the bravest thing we can do is to pray and wait.

Think
Where do you need to find strength in the waiting?

Sanctification

"May God himself, the God of peace, sanctify you through and through. May your whole spirit, soul and body be kept blameless at the coming of our Lord Jesus Christ." 1 Thessalonians 5:23

Sanctification sounds like a cool, beautiful, "religious" word. It reminds me of church steeples, stained glass windows, and hushed pews with sacred prayers. If you look up the word's definition, it means simply being made or becoming holy. It sounds like something I definitely want.

In truth, it's messy, difficult, and uncomfortable. In practice, it is more like pruning, pricking and confessing. In real life, it's where the rubber of your faith meets the road of life.

To me, personal sanctification is looking at my life through the lens of Jesus and asking what needs realignment. Lately, God is pointing things out, pruning and convicting me more than I want. To be honest, I don't like it. However, if I am truly living the Christian walk, I need to be uncomfortable as I seek more to be like Jesus.

I like being comfortable. I like achievement, doing good things, and working hard to succeed at life. On their own, these are good things. However, God wants our very best. He didn't put us on the earth so we could simply learn a bunch of stuff, get our kids into a quality college, and secure fantastic jobs so we can earn a lot of money to buy a bunch more stuff.

Yet when I look at my daily actions, it looks like I'm working hard at achieving exactly those things. I do want goodness for my child, but I want him to want Jesus more. Do my daily actions in my homeschool provide evidence I'm working hard at Jesus or working hard at getting more stuff?

If my purpose is to get Jesus right as the main point of homeschooling, it makes my heart hurt a little bit. It makes me wonder why I'm so anxious about Latin and SAT scores and activities for my child to put on his college application. It calls me out on all my busy-ness to whisper, "Those things don't really matter."

People always told me if you raise a virtuous child, everything else will fall into place. If you can encourage their hearts to be aligned with Jesus and focused on kingdom-style things, they will have a well-lived life. This may not include admittance to a popular university, work for a Fortune 500 company, or solve important problems in the world. All those things would be amazing. But God, in His creative ways, always surprises us in what "very best" might look like.

I can see that if my child struggles, he can pray and trust in Jesus to see him through. If my child has moral choices to make, he can look to Jesus for direction. If he is struggling with a job or relationship or character issues, he can look to Jesus and the Bible for understanding. If he gets sick, or if he needs community, friendship, or encouragement, he can seek Jesus and His church for the support he needs. If you go down the list of every potential life challenge, Jesus is always the answer and the point.

I'm not saying all the quality academic work we do isn't important. I love Latin, the challenge of the sciences, and I have made friends with math. I treasure enriching extracurricular activities and volunteer work and meaningful field trips. I love it all. But I love Jesus more. I have come to understand through pruning and pricking, nothing else really matters in your homeschool except getting Jesus right. It's been a hard lesson. The journey of sanctification is still ongoing in me.

Think
How are you making Jesus front and center in your homeschool?

Making Friends with Defeat

"But they who wait for the Lord shall renew their strength; they shall mount up with wings like eagles; they shall run and not be weary; they shall walk and not faint." Isaiah 40:31

I hate building character.

We used to have an ice hockey coach who would always match us up for games with teams that were way beyond our ability. He always presented it as some high honor to play this fantastic team. As a parent, I hated it. "Here is the chance to get creamed," I used to think. Or better yet, "Here's our chance to build character."

I don't want any more character. I have enough character. Why do I have to be crushed in order to grow? Why can't I simply study it, read about it, understand it and then move on to the good stuff in life? Why do I have to be defeated and discouraged in order to be a better human?

As a parent, I get it. Failure is a great idea, except when it's your kid. In my heart I want to do everything I can to help my kid avoid failure. But luckily, life provides plenty of opportunities for all of us to practice defeat.

In all of our failures, I'm learning to trust God. I know if we were able to do everything in our own abilities, we wouldn't need a Savior. We would make ourselves little gods, letting our ego and our achievements be our satisfaction. But through failure, disappointment, defeat, and discouragement, we learn about resilience. It is through relying on our Savior instead of our own abilities we learn about trust. It is through hardship and sacrifice of self, we learn about faith.

Jesus could have come to earth as a king. He could have lived in a palace with successes, wealth, treasure, and all the good things. But He willingly gave it all up for us. He sacrificed all the things of the world, in order to cover all of our failures, disappointments and sins. He showed us failure isn't final and that we are not defined by our earthly treasure or our worldly achievements.

When we fail, we grow. When we are broken, we can then be used by God. Trust is the same way. When we have run out of fulfillment and contentment in our stuff and our ego, then we are ready to trust in Jesus. It's the upside-down nature of our faith. Jesus died so we can truly live. He took our place in condemnation, so we could have life in abundance.

When you look at it like that, it makes you hungry to risk more for Jesus. It makes you want to go all out in your faith walk. It makes you want to fail more, give of yourself more, be more for Jesus. It makes you want to celebrate defeat and discouragement, so you can be reminded of why we need Jesus in everything.

Think
Where are you facing defeat? How can you reframe that defeat to sink deeper into Jesus?

Finding Hope in Sleepless Nights

"In peace I will lie down and sleep, for you alone, Lord, make me dwell in safety." Psalm 4:8

Sleepless nights have been my constant companion.

Through the years of homeschooling, my sleepless nights would come and go. With each new season of homeschooling, a fresh worry would surface in my thoughts. When am I supposed to sign up for the PSAT? How do you weigh courses on your transcript for honors, community college or AP level? Is anyone even going to look at a transcript? Did I leave the crockpot on?

My thoughts would not stop.

A friend of mine once told me that when God wakes you up in the middle of the night, it means He wants to have a word with you. If that is true, then God has lots of words He wants to share with me. I used to get frustrated over my inability to sleep. However, if my friend was right and God really wanted to have a word with me, I needed to at least listen, or at least try.

Instead of getting irritated, I decided I would pray. I would always start with the oldest people in my family and pray over their health and joy for all the days that remain. I would work my way by age through siblings, in-laws, nieces, nephews, cousins, neighbors, and friends. Usually, I wouldn't get very far in my praying before I somehow drifted back to sleep. Combing through my family members with thoughts of covering prayers was nurturing to me. It shifted my mind from worry to love.

Now when I find myself awake in the middle of the night it feels like a sacred space. The house is draped in quiet. Sometimes, I have a cup of tea or quietly meditate on what God might want to say to me at this hour. I think of other parents and friends who may be awake with me in this lonely window. Mostly I think of it as the time for God to share with me without the distractions of the day.

Sleepless nights are still regular times for me. I try to make friends with my racing mind, wild emotions, and endless mental frittering. When I am able to shift my thinking from frenzy to an attitude of prayer and reflection, something quiets in me. As I consider it a chance to approach the throne and hear God in the quiet moments, it becomes a holy place.

Covering others in prayer takes the focus off of myself and shifts it to considering others. In truth, there will always be something to worry over, no matter the season of life. Sleepless nights are now my invitation to pray and spend time with God.

Think
When you have a sleepless night, how can you reframe it for good?

Blooming in Secret

"For you died, and your life is now hidden with Christ in God." Colossians 3:3

Sometimes it feels like your homeschool is invisible. Tucked away and hidden, usually no one but your family witnesses your dedicated homeschool efforts.

When I caught a glimpse of daffodils blooming on a tucked away hillside, I was reminded of this notion. They were early blooms and it was miraculous that I spotted them at all. They were down a steep bank, way off the road, barely visible from anywhere. Yet, there they were blooming like crazy. No one would ever notice their beauty except for a rare passerby, like me.

At times, your homeschooling efforts can feel like the hidden daffodils. We do all of this work to provide a rich feast of ideas. We surround ourselves with quality resources and align our hearts and minds with lofty intentions. Like the secret blooms, we prepare rich soil, optimum lighting conditions, and nourishment for growth.

Then we hope and wait for blooms to burst forth. Nurturing, watering, encouraging, protecting, disciplining, and coaching. We do all of it until, finally, we see the blooms. Other than our own family, no one else has any idea of the beauty and goodness we work so hard to create in home-schooling.

I know we don't homeschool for the attention and acco-lades, but I sometimes long for affirmation that I'm doing it well. Watching your child master a hard concept is a pretty satisfying reward. You observe their struggle day by day and finally witness the moment when they understand a hard-fought idea. We see them in their daily self-esteem battles, their social upsets, and their precarious navigation of the teen years with the rollercoaster ride of emotions. We see them working hard at becoming who God wants them to be.

We watch, we love, we wait. We pray for God to make His presence known in their life. With desperate hearts, we pray for God to show up and to keep showing up in bold ways. We cling to the hope and prayer that our children will follow hard after Him all of the days of their lives. We do all the things we know to do, then we anxiously release them to God, allowing Him to take them from here.

The Bible assures us He will. But in the releasing, trusting and waiting, we traverse deep waters of agony to beg Him to show up. We long to see the buds of blossoms to affirm that God is at work, that He is planting within them all the plans for their lives. We long for them to bloom.

Your heart searches for any signs of promise. You keep going, doing the only thing you can do: keep showing up and keep searching for goodness. Then one day, when we least expect it, it happens. That is when the bloom bursts forth -- unexpectedly, unequivocally, on a quiet spot on a hillside. It's a secret bloom that shows up for you alone, because God knows only you will see it.

All of the love you have poured in can't help but pour out. It may take time, patience, watching, and waiting in Him. He will show up. Trust that the blooms will come at exactly the right time.

<u>Think</u>
Where are you seeing blooms of growth in your homeschool?

Move Past Your Emotions

"Dear friend, I pray that you may enjoy good health and that all may go well with you, even as your soul is getting along well." 3 John 1:2

Walking in the fresh air heals me.

Recently, the sun was not even up and anxiety was already pulsing in my heart. I knew what I needed to do: put on my sneakers and head out the door. With praise and worship blasting in my headphones, being in motion felt like I'm doing something helpful to change.

The act of moving my body vigorously through the streets and hills invites a soothing tone over my morning. Changing my environment by getting outside tames the natty places in my heart and mind. I invite Jesus to be close. I plead for God to help me find a way through this day. I seek His face first in the desire that He can carry me through.

With the hope of Jesus in my heart, I don't understand how these feelings rule my thoughts. If I'm a Christian that follows Jesus, shouldn't I be able to handle these things better? Sometimes my emotions can hijack my spirit. I do the only things I know to do that make me feel better. I read the Bible, pray, write in my journal, and keep moving.

I wonder how people like Moses, David, Joshua, Mary, and Esther handled days when they felt like they couldn't get past their feelings. I know they were human like me and also struggling with their own insecurities. I wonder how they moved from feeling inadequate to walking and trusting with joy. I'm sure, like me, they did the only thing they knew how to do, seek God.

There are days in homeschooling when I am confident of what we are doing. The day takes on a steady rhythm of order with an assurance in the work that is to be done. Then there are the days when I wake up and wonder how I am going to get through this day. Those are the days when I question every decision and simple tasks feel harder than they need to be.

I think the answer is to keep going. Even when I'm struggling, I need to set aside the emotions and keep seeking God. On those days, I do the next thing. I give myself armfuls of grace. I allow myself to rest, and then I keep going. I acknowledge how I am feeling, but that these feelings do not define me.

On those days, I need to ask for help. This might be through prayers, spending more time with God, sending my son to handle errands or the laundry for me. On those days, I need to practice letting go of trying to do too many things. I invite others in to share the load. I have to be okay with needing help and support sometimes. As a person who loves to help others and doesn't like to need help, this is particularly difficult for me.

When I'm finished working off my anxiety, I find a stillness settling in my heart. These anxious feelings are a reminder to look deeper. I ask God to show me what I need to see in this moment. Perhaps this emotional day is God's reminder that others can take over at times, too. This personal timeout is a chance for others to practice ministry right at home. Perhaps this is God's way of telling me it is perfectly okay to ask for the love and grace I need.

Think
How can you invite others to care for you at times?

Transcripts Are Not the Boss of Me

"If any of you lacks wisdom, you should ask God, who gives generously to all without finding fault, and it will be given to you." James 1:5

Transcripts, you are not the boss of me.

I have seen my fair share of parents quit homeschooling over creating a transcript. I get it. It seems overwhelming with assigning grades and figuring out a weighting system for different classes. Figuring out how to demonstrate all of your child's history on one piece of paper is a lot of pressure.

When I wanted to hyperventilate over grades and transcripts, a wise friend came alongside me and said, "Don't let that be the hill you die on."

Transcripts can be figured out. They only take a little time and attention. It doesn't have to be done all at once. Working on it little by little over time helped me to stay positive and to understand things as I went. I certainly could have opted for fancier versions by paying someone to help me prepare it. I also could have invested in a software program that would prepare all of it for me. Instead, I made a basic document with lists of classes and grades as I went. I tried every style of transcript over the years and for me, the simplest was the best.

After using fancy software programs for a while and getting frustrated, I simply decided to list everything in a document. It wasn't elaborate or organized. All I was trying to do was to capture what the class was, when my child took it, a description of what he studied, textbooks and books they used and anything significant I wanted to highlight as part of the class itself. I added in a section for grades and any notes I wanted to include about the class. If it was taught by a co-op, college or instructor, I listed the name and organization as part of the class.

Extracurricular activities and service were listed as well, including years of participation, and any special achievements as part of each of the activities. Capturing the amount of service hours was valuable as well. Don't trust your memory and while it is fresh, write down anything significant from the year in your transcript notes.

When I was working on transcripts, I found a couple of friends with similar mindsets and goals. Having someone to collaborate with was life-giving and confidence boosting. We collaborated by sharing ideas, grading insights, and styles of transcripts. We looked over each other's documents, gave feed-back, and made suggestions. My friend, Diana did this for me and we encouraged each other in making our transcripts the best they could be.

We both did some research on weighting classes according to our states and calculating grade point averages. By discussing and sharing our ideas together, as well as reviewing each other's final transcripts, we felt our finished products represented the highest integrity of our homeschools.

Find a friend or two with whom you can collaborate with on your transcripts that can help you present your children's accomplishments in the best possible light. I wanted to be sensitive about my son's grades and test scores being shared, so we worked together on the overall template and then I entered his scores later. It's a good idea to be transparent with your child on sharing their transcript and honoring their wishes. As a matter of respect, I felt like it was important to protect hearts and minds in the process.

It takes a community to homeschool well. It also takes a community to document and present your homeschool to the world well. Finding like-minded friends to partner with you will sharpen your transcript to be the best it can be. You can do it, with a little time and dedication. Don't let that silly piece of paper be the boss of you.

Think
Who can you collaborate with for support as you prepare transcripts and academic documents?

5

Renewal
CHAPTER FIVE

Ideas and inspiration for finding refreshment in the homeschool season.

"Do not conform to the pattern of this world, but be transformed by the renewing of your mind. Then you will be able to test and approve what God's will is— his good, pleasing and perfect will."
Romans 12:2

Resting as You Go

"Come to me, all you who are weary and burdened, and I will give you rest. Take my yoke upon you and learn from me, for I am gentle and humble in heart, and you will find rest for your souls. For my yoke is easy and my burden is light." Matthew 11:28-30

Veteran homeschoolers encouraged me to "teach from a place of rest." My first response was, "I don't have time for that."

Busy was my badge of honor and tired was my accomplishment. An overfull life was my trophy to prove I was homeschooling well. I struggled to find rest in the busy seasons of homeschooling because busy in my heart meant worthwhile.

I was confusing rest with a vacation. My understanding of rest was limited to a weeklong vacation in the Caribbean. It was only for the one or two weeks a year when we were able to get away from it all. Rest definitely can be time spent on an island or napping at the beach. More than that, real rest doesn't require packing a suitcase, it only requires knowing rest is allowed even when the work isn't done.

More than vacations, I knew I needed to shift my view of

rest. I wanted to find rest woven into the everyday moments for replenishment. Pockets of rest could be discovered over a cup of tea before the day began. By taking time to exercise or walk, restful moments were available to me every day. Resting as I went in homeschooling was a life-giving idea I longed to put into practice.

For starters, I began looking at my days. What does God have in store for me this week? What would I like the focus of my time to be this week? How can I fill my week with things that are soul-enriching and on purpose? Instead of always reacting to the schedule, how could I design my day with care? How can I make room for God in my week? If every space of my day is filled, how am I available for what God has planned for me? Blank spaces as part of my schedule were newfound gifts for rest, listening, and hearing God's plans.

Busy doesn't mean worthy. A good life can look quiet and ordinary on the outside. Days for which nothing is planned can be equally as wonderful as days chockfull of activity. Sometimes the best days are those when nothing is planned at all.

The heart and soul of your homeschool starts with you. Live your days in such a way that shows your kids a well-lived life. Your kids watch everything you do. Show them what a passionate, God-loving parent looks like. This doesn't necessarily mean a busy parent, but one who knows how to live well and rest well. Teach them that saying "no" to good things sometimes leads to the very best things. Model for them that God speaks to us in the pauses and spaces. This starts with first having room in our lives to hear Him.

Think
How can you put pauses for rest in each day? How can you replenish as you go?

Right Now Joy

"A cheerful heart is good medicine..." Proverbs 17:22

I love listening to podcasts. One of my favorite podcasts closes every episode by asking the question, "What is giving you joy right now?"

Inevitably, listeners share something inspiring like a neat book, a favorite app, a daily habit or a ritual they have started incorporating into their day. Every time I listen to that question, it immediately invites me to turn to my own life and wonder, "What is giving me joy right now?"

This question reminds me of water towers. I have a friend with a special needs brother who is obsessed with water towers. Whenever I see him, he asks me if I know of the water tower near my hometown, or of a water tower where I went to college, or the water tower near an airport. From memory, he can describe almost every water tower style, color, and shape with exact details. After spending several days in a row with him, our family, too, became obsessed with water towers.

Soon after, our family travelled to Michigan and during our drive across the state, we could not help but shout out with jubilation, "Water tower!" every time we saw a new one. Those water towers had always been there, but because of my friend's passion, it carried over to our hearts as a source of passion, too.

Joy is like that. It's always there for the finding. Sometimes when I'm having a terrible day, I remind myself of the same important question, "What is giving me joy right now?" It is still there, waiting to be noticed yet again.

For me, joy has been going for walks and truly noticing the season. The colors have been changing so softly, you could miss them if you don't pay attention. On a recent walk, I closed my eyes and took a deep breath to capture the fall smells. I noticed the tumbling leaves falling like confetti and swirling in tiny tornadoes. I listened for the sounds of travelling birds. I admired the artistic long shadow created by my silhouette. I loved how the sun's rays were changing in the fading golden light.

Homeschooling through high school can be a grind. I see families with younger children and I feel a deep nostalgia. I miss the days of abundant field trips, reading lovely picture books together and being more deeply involved in the rich feast of learning. Now my role has shifted to serving as more of a project manager and a quality control inspector.

I find myself immersed in college-prep planning, transcript tracking and accounting-style activities. Even though this season has a different focus, there is still joy to be found. My days may have an ordinary rhythm, but there is still goodness in it.

When you think about joy this way, you realize it's everywhere. It's not only in the mountaintop moments when your student writes an excellent paper or shares a profound speech. It's found in the dinnertime moments when your kids ask you what you were like in high school or want to know your thoughts about careers at their age. It's found in car rides to the grocery store and folding laundry while discussing the news. It is like water towers. It is everywhere. There is so much of it, you can't help but open your eyes and be overwhelmed by seeing God's joy everywhere you look.

Think
What is giving you joy right now?

Treasuring Community

"For just as each of us has one body with many members, and these members do not all have the same function, so in Christ we, though many, form one body, and each member belongs to all the others." Romans 12:4-5

Homeschooling works best in community.

In the early days of homeschooling, our family met weekly on Thursdays as part of a classical community. I loved Thursdays. During those early seasons of elementary and middle school, we would sit in tiny classrooms to share a common curriculum. During our lunch break when the weather was nice, we would spread out blankets on the church's lawn under a tree in the sunshine. On days when it wasn't nice weather, we gathered in the church's fellowship hall and shared lunch, swapped ideas, and stories. We laughed about the funny way we remember Latin declensions or that we can't stop thinking about skip counting math in our sleep.

When we got home from community day, we were exhausted. Still, it was a good kind of exhausted. We had worked hard and fellowshipped deeply with homeschooling friends. Then we would hunker down for the rest of the school week to work through the materials in our own style and at our own pace, until we did it all again next Thursday.

As we aged up in homeschooling, our community changed too. For high school, our life became a mixed bag of learning. We had a variety of virtual classes, community college classes, test prep classes, work, volunteering, and extracurricular activities. My son was travelling to his various classes and activities without me, changing our community dynamic again.

The high school years can be lonely ones for parents. As my student aged up, he began to need me less and less. This was exactly as it was supposed to be, but I missed the connection of community. Along with more independence, this meant other parents were less involved and therefore fewer opportunities to connect. I soon realized how important it was to continue to foster friendships and community in changing seasons.

Community sometimes requires effort, but it is worth it. For me, we found active community experiences through extracurricular activities such as the Science Olympiad team, academic clubs like the Honor Society, and sports teams. We would also collaborate intentionally and swap ideas on good classes, teachers, SAT/ACT prep, and college essays. Sometimes, we would invent mini workshops on college applications and personal finance. Other times we would get together as parents to fellowship and share our hearts over coffee or lunch or a walk.

For student fellowship, plugging into a high school church youth group was the best decision. My son made lifelong friends through camps, socials, events, and church experiences. At home, we would host game nights, movie nights and holiday parties. Find other like-minded friends who understand the importance of fellowship and community.

We have just a handful of years with our high school kids and then hopefully, they launch into the world. Our family decided to do all we could to foster a healthy and vibrant community for our son and his friends. Community can become a source of light, encouragement, and joy for your family. Don't journey the homeschooling path alone. Find others who will support you along the way. It is a worthy path that is best treasured with community.

<u>Think</u>
How can you be intentional about community?

"And we all, who with unveiled faces contemplate the Lord's glory, are being transformed into his image with ever-increasing glory, which comes from the Lord, who is the Spirit." 2 Corinthians 3:18

What we behold, we become.

I've been reading a book called, *Beholding and Becoming: The Art of Everyday Worship*[1] by Ruth Chou Simons that speaks to the everyday walk of our Christian lives. Her encouragement is that we have a chance each day to be more like Jesus with our ordinary worship through what we behold.

This makes perfect sense to me. In homeschooling, my temptation is to make my daily worship about accomplishing. In this framework, my worship is about something of this world, not Jesus. When I start my day with anything else but prayer and spending time in the Word, the day doesn't feel quite right. The quiet time aligns my heart. My hope is not to make it a spiritual checklist. My hope is to make it a chance to abide deeply in His love to start the day.

Each day is a chance to become a shade more like Jesus. I

have gone through different seasons of reading the Word, not understanding the Word, being on fire about the Word, and being frustrated by the Word. But I know that even if I read only one sentence from the Bible a day, it changes me. It allows me to connect to a holy part of myself that is of God. There is always something good to be found by spending time in the Word and talking to God daily.

Sometimes I journal my prayers, sometimes I copy scripture, sometimes I use a phone app as a devotion, other times I use a devotional book. There are days I pray out loud and days I sit quietly and feel like I need to listen. I sometimes work through a formal Bible study, spending weeks or months on a single chapter of the Bible. Other times, I bounce around to something that I am searching for in a particular scripture. On busy days, I will look at a single sentence of the Word. When I am desperate for God, I crank up the praise and worship music or put on an inspirational podcast to give me more spiritual food for my day.

Lately, I have felt like I'm in a season of being hungry for more of God. I want to understand Him in a deeper way. I hope He will continue to keep me hungry for more of Him and pressing into Him. There is always something new to discover in Him, if we are consistent in seeking Him.

My gentle encouragement is to consider what you behold first each day. For me, I don't want my phone to be what I behold first each day. I don't want my spiritual checklists to be what I behold each day. I want God alone to be what I behold to start my day. Our God is such a personal God, who speaks to us exactly where we meet Him. I hope God will continue to stir up my heart to fall deeper in love with Him each day. I want each day to bring new discoveries about Him. My desire is to behold more of His goodness every morning, so that I am growing one shade closer to Jesus' idea of me. My hope is to behold Him and His promises, so I can honor His will for my life.

<u>Think</u>
What are you beholding first each day?

Playing the Cool Parent Card

"I praise you because I am fearfully and wonderfully made; your works are wonderful, I know that full well." Psalm 139:14

Every once in a while, I play the "cool parent" card.

When I say "cool parent" card, I mean finding the right moment to give abundant grace, forgiveness, or joy when there is no real reason for it. This does not come naturally to me. In my case, I need to be intentional about finding the perfect moment to play it.

During my son's senior year, our family was preparing to head out on a spring vacation. Because homeschool schedules don't always break precisely at the same time, one of my son's classes was still meeting and had homework deadlines all week. My son had a couple of hours of homework due each day during his vacation week, even though he was technically on vacation.

I decided to play the cool parent card and emailed the teacher to ask if my son could take his spring break earlier instead of when it was scheduled. We committed to turn in his homework the following week when the rest of the class had their spring break. His instructor graciously agreed and I became the cool parent for my son.

Your cool parent card play may be different according to what would be meaningful for your child. A break from the routine, a get out of an assignment free, a special treat or meal, or anything that simply says, "You are loved. Here is some grace to remind you that you don't have to earn it."

Some days I was tired of being at home. To give everyone a break, I would say, "Let's get in the car and get cheese-burgers for lunch." We would grab our drive-through lunch and find a nearby park. We would find a sunny spot and spread out our fun lunch and sit in folding chairs. On those days, with joy as our intention, our conversations were relaxed, easy going, and from the heart. Some of the best conversations were held over quick car rides and cheese-burgers.

I wasn't playing the cool parent card to be my son's best friend. I was doing it for the opportunity to surprise and delight him with something good. Isn't that what God's good-ness is like? He surprises and delights us in unexpected ways and exactly when we need encouragement.

At times it was hard for me to give abundant grace to my child because of my limited view. In my mind, grace was in finite supply. I rationalized if I doled it out all the time, it wouldn't be special or we would use it up. I'm not saying we have to treat our children all the time.

However, taking the time to demonstrate we see them in the midst of their struggles can be a lovely blessing. God is a personal God, who loves us in ways that are unique to every person. From that kind of love, we can pour out our specific love to our family, in meaningful ways to them.

I hope you will find ways to lavish love on your child during this season. For high school, you get four years to surround them with the love and blessings only a King could inspire. From the source of matchless care, we are able to pour out this love because He first loved us.

<u>Think</u>
What are some creative ways you can demonstrate God's grace to your child this week?

Sabbath

"I am the Lord your God; follow my decrees and be careful to keep my laws. Keep my Sabbaths holy, that they may be a sign between us. Then you will know that I am the Lord your God." Ezekiel 20:19-20

Taking a day of rest doesn't have to happen only on Sundays.

I used to get frustrated when the neighborhood kids in traditional school had teacher workdays. Inevitably, by mid-morning we would hear them outside whooping it up. Soon enough they would be ringing our doorbell to ask if my son could toss a Frisbee or shoot hoops. Since we schooled at home, they knew the chances of him being home were high.

Like Cinderella who was left at home during the royal ball, my child felt like he was sentenced to infinite amounts of hard labor while everyone else was having fun. Snow days were even worse. It's pretty hard to focus when there's a party going on in your front yard.

As my child got older and knew what needed to get done, this became easier. I let him make the decision for his time. Did he want to work for an hour to make some progress and then go have some fun? Or did he want to hunker down so that he could have the afternoon free to goof off without worrying about school.

Schooling at home means we can be efficient with our time. The difficult thing about homeschooling is the work is always there. We don't take teacher workdays, or in-service days or truly even snow days. We can always get work done.

I remember listening to a teaching about homeschooling that encouraged the idea of "goofing off first." With my check box, get it done, Type A personality, this felt really uncomfortable to me. If we goof off first, we might not get all our work done. If we don't get our work done, we may not accomplish anything. If we don't accomplish anything, we won't have anything to show for our day. Goofing off first sounded reckless and unproductive. Or could it be a genius way to approach the day with fun and lightheartedness?

God created the Sabbath to encourage us and to show us breaks are necessary. Let's face it, He's God and didn't need to rest. Still, He gave us the Sabbath to model for us that rest is important and good. Taking time to rest, renew, and recharge is vital for the health and wellness of your family.

When I learned to relax more about school, I let my student decide what he wanted to do with his day. Sometimes he wasted it. Sometimes he was productive. I had to be okay with the result. Becoming an adult means letting life be the teacher even when the lessons are hard.

I could have nagged him or required him to finish his homework first. Instead, I allowed him to decide his day. As parents, we can certainly hold a high standard for our children for what a good choice looks like. But it is also a chance for them to practice what their personal rhythm of work, play, goofing off, and Sabbath looks like for them, too.

One day they will have to do all of it on their own. If they already know what their best rhythm looks like, they are more likely to own it. Rest is equally as important as productivity.

Finding the ideal balance of work, goofing off and rest can be life-giving for your family.

<u>Think</u>

How can you encourage your child to develop their own rhythm of productivity, rest, and fun for their school?

Blooming Anyway

"Consider how the wild flowers grow. They do not labor or spin. Yet I tell you, not even Solomon in all his splendor was dressed like one of these." Luke 12:27

"It's spring! How are you blooming?"

I read that line and my first reaction was to roll my eyes at the cheery expression. Yet, I want to bloom. Booming is something that happens after all the hard work is done. With the right care and efforts, blooming happens almost effortlessly.

I recently found a packet of lavender seeds. One Saturday several weeks ago, I decided I would plant them in a pot. I found a lovely container hidden in my garage, poured in some really rich soil, layered the seeds in the soil, and carefully covered them with mulch. When I remembered, I watered my humble pot. Then I left it alone and forgot about it.

Yesterday, I was walking around the yard and discovered beautiful tiny lavender shoots bursting through the soil. To see the tiny buds pushing forth felt like an unexpected gift after a long, hard day.

I think blooming is about noticing. It's putting in a good-faith effort and then waiting for time to reveal the beautiful shoots of your efforts. Truly it's about love and patience -- two fantastic qualities to honor in the homeschooling walk. Every season provides an opportunity to think about what is working well, what is not working well, and where you are seeing "blooms" of progress in your homeschooling season.

Every year God surprises me in new ways. Even when I fail miserably -- when we don't finish the book, when something is forgotten, or when we mess up on math -- He still is there, teaching a new lesson in perseverance, trust, and growing anyway. Even when our efforts fall short according to the world's standards, we bloom anyway. Sometimes the "falling short" is the bloom.

I think about the miracle of my lavender pot. I did a couple of things well and I let time do the rest. Despite my lack of effort, my lavender bloomed anyway. As you think through this homeschooling season, take a moment to pause and notice. Where is your student blooming, anyway? Where are you blooming anyway? How is God showing you that your loving efforts are still yielding?

My invitation for you is to take some time to admire the blooms. Recognize your humble efforts are producing something beautiful in the name of our Father. Blooming allows us the chance to praise God for His faithful love, to celebrate the efforts of time well spent. Best of all, it is our chance to remember, regardless of how imperfect we are, God is faithful. He allows us to bloom anyway.

Think
Where are you blooming anyway?

Hidden Places

"The Lord will guide you always; he will satisfy your needs in a sun-scorched land and will strengthen your frame. You will be like a well-watered garden, like a spring whose waters never fail." Isaiah 58:11

I once slept in a castle in Ireland. Our neighbor's son was getting married and his bride-to-be was a native of Ireland. With over 300 castles throughout the country, we decided it would be a once-in-a-lifetime experience to sleep in one.

The castle did not disappoint us with its vast legends, lore, and dramatic history. As we were packing to leave and head on to our next destination, the castle host asked me if I had visited the garden. I had not. With our go-go American agenda, I had been so busy seeing the sights I hadn't walked to the backyard. He said that I absolutely had to see it before I left. He insisted.

I hesitated since everyone was preparing to leave and my bags were literally on the front porch, or in this case, the front moat. Yet something in his insistence forced me to go. Reluctantly and obligingly, I went.

Around back, a small *Alice-in-Wonderland* style door was

framed by a rock wall, centuries old. It appeared simple, a tiny passageway. Stooping through the frame, I was astonished by what I saw. As I entered the tiny unassuming door, several acres literally unfolded before me presenting tumbling flowers, elaborate statues, pebbled footpaths, archways, pergolas, and plants towering above and below me. Gorgeous beauty was everywhere I looked. It was stunning.

I think back on that moment and wondered, "What if I had missed it?" What if I had been so busy that I didn't take five minutes to see the backyard? In hindsight, that garden surprise was one of the highlights of the of the entire trip.

Here at home, I have a tiny garden that is often neglected and overgrown. Usually during the spring season, I start to dream of the possibilities. I consider what could grow as I gather seeds and peruse the garden center. I love the idea of gardening, but I struggle with making time for it. Everything in the high school and homeschooling world feels more important -- college visits, SAT prep, reviewing papers, discussing books, making checklists of to-dos and so on.

If I'm not careful, I can let homeschooling become more important than anything else. Sometimes I am guilty of being so busy, that I neglect my own health, friendships, spouse, faith, and my own passions. It's so easy to let homeschooling become the most important thing.

When I find myself in "overdoing" mode, I look to my little garden. Just walking outside and spending time clearing weeds reminds me of the dreams still inside of me. I can simply trim a few clippings or spend time raking a patch. It untangles the knotted places in my heart. It reminds me of the real me. The one God loves and wants to spend time with every day. The one that is full of dreams and hopes and desires beyond the list of to-dos. It reminds me I am more than my "doings."

My encouragement to you as a homeschooling parent is to find your secret garden. Find the thing that allows you to tend to your soul, the thing that undoes the fears, worries, and knotty places in you. Gardening may not be your thing. Perhaps it's cooking, handcrafts, reading poetry, journaling, or walking in nature. Whatever it may be for you, make time on a regular basis to tend the secret place in you.

Our children need us to be parents who know the love of the Creator by experiencing it firsthand. When we are filled with this kind of love, we can't help but pour out on our families and our pursuits. We must tend the secret gardens of our soul in order to fully bloom in life.

Think
How are you caring for and nurturing yourself during this homeschooling journey?

Easier

"Enter his gates with thanksgiving and his courts with praise; give thanks to him and praise his name. For the Lord is good and his love endures forever; his faithfulness continues through all generations." Psalm 100:4-5

"Snapping makes things easier."

This nugget of wisdom was shared with me recently during an exercise class. We were all struggling to hold a position of sitting against a wall on an invisible chair. The instructor perkily suggested, "If you snap while you do hold the position, it goes quicker. Snapping pretty much makes everything easier. Try it!"

Unconvinced, I thought I would test it out. Really? Could a simple thing like a snap make life easier?

Short answer: Yes.

This made me wonder why it works. There I was, suspended in my air chair, with a horrible look on my face. Listening to the song playing in the background, I snapped to the tune of the bouncy beat. Not only did it take my mind off the painful task, it also allowed me to enjoy the song. Snapping is actually quite fun. I was able to do the hard thing longer and enjoy the moment.

This idea invited me to consider if there are other things that make life easier by simply applying a fun trick? I started thinking about applying this mental shift for tasks I loathe. What "snaps" could I apply to these things, too? What were little things I could do to make difficult tasks easier?

When I am irritated by my child wasting his time, I could pray over him and invite him to finish up early so we could do something he loves.

When I'm overwhelmed by what to make for dinner, I can prep or plan over the weekend when I have more time and mental energy. I can task my child with dinner, or, I can order pizza.

When my child is filled with drama or overreacting to life, I can calmly choose not to react and instead choose something healthy such a taking a walk, reading a devotion, or calling a friend for support.

When I'm feeling maxed out and stressed, I can decide to stop. I can give myself permission to take a nap or go to the library to read magazines, have coffee with a friend, or do something that feels rejuvenating.

When I feel lonely for friends, my spouse or desire anything but being a homeschool parent, I can pray for God to come closer and to make His presence known to me.

Snapping by itself isn't revolutionary. What it does is reframe the hard thing in such a way to make it more pleasurable. When you search for ways to make the difficult in your life to become more joy-filled, they become more joy-filled. Or at least a bit better, or snappier in this case.

Ask God to show you how to find joy in the hard things.

Think
How can you reframe hard things to make them more joy-filled?

Hiving Off

"Accept one another, then, just as Christ accepted you, in order to bring praise to God." Romans 15:7

"Be careful not to hive yourself off," a friend recently shared. I had no idea what she meant in her cautionary tone.

She shared that "hiving off" is when we get stuck in the rut of the same circle of friends, activities, or things. We get stuck in our own "hives" if you will.

This can easily happen in homeschooling. I could see how it was already happening in certain aspects of my own home-school life. Almost all of our classes, the church we attend, my son's friend group, my friends' get-togethers were all within my own "hive."

Let's face it, it's easy to be with your own hive mates. They understand where you are and the struggles you face. There is a lot to talk about and to share when you are with people who deeply get you and know your situation. However, the problem with hiving off is that you may miss opportunities for growth.

There came a point when everything I did was only in the

homeschooling community and only with homeschooling friends. It was never my intention to be limited this way; it was simply a natural extension of the life I had created.

As homeschoolers, it's important to be intentional in being about more than just homeschooling things. If we only think in the homeschooling dimension, we are missing out on opportunities.

We have so much to learn from different voices and different generations. I recently went to a Women's Connect event at my church and was able to sit with a grandmother. She shared what her days were like and her insights offered me a glimpse of what things might look like when my home-schooling days are over. Across the table sat a trio of young moms, thick in the days of birthing, child rearing, and potty training. Despite their cute outfits, I could tell they were tired from lack of sleep and constant going. Yet they held an excited relief to be out of the home for an evening. They were desperate for encouragement and knowing what my life was like with a high schooler.

Now that my child is becoming more independent, I am not needed as much to help manage his days. I have more freedom to practice what my life might look like beyond homeschooling. This comes at a vital time for me as I am craving fresh voices, viewpoints, and experiences.

My child needs to see what a parent looks like who has passions and interests beyond the home and beyond home-schooling. He needs to see I can also pursue learning and life outside of his world, too. Our children need to see what an adult with dynamic intentions looks like. Find things you are interested in learning about and passions beyond home-schooling.

It's vital to surround ourselves with enrichment beyond homeschool priorities. Live a full life to includes fresh voices, fresh stages, and fresh experiences.

<u>Think</u>
How can you be intentional with your own connections and interests?

```
┌─────────────────────────────────┐
│                                 │
│            Pauses               │
│                                 │
└─────────────────────────────────┘
```

"...not looking to your own interests but each of you to the interests of the others." Philippians 2:4

Tuesdays have become "lunch date" days with my son.

On this day each week, we make it a point to go grab lunch out of the house, a rare treat. This wasn't planned with grand intentions. The idea of "date lunch" happened one day when I was sick of being in the house.

Knowing there isn't a teenager alive who doesn't love fast food, I asked my son if he wanted to take a break and go grab lunch. With a huge smile and a vibrant, "Absolutely!" we got in the car and went through the drive through at his favorite restaurant.

I happened to have two camping chairs in the car and it was a pretty day, so we decided to take our fast food picnic to a local park. We sat outside enjoying the sunshine and talking. Actually, he did most of the talking and I practiced listening. My tendency is to ask a lot of questions like, "Did you do this?" or "Have you done that, yet?" or "What about that thing I asked you to do last week?"

I gave my questions a rest. I let him do the talking. If he

didn't talk, I let the space be filled with the beauty and quiet of a gorgeous day. I pointed out the lovely things around us. I was present to the moment of a mom and her son having lunch on a sunny Tuesday.

Since then, it's become a weekly tradition. It is not hard and fast with a "have to" or "we need to do this" mindset. It is more a free, lightly-held fun thing when I casually ask, "Do you want to grab lunch?"

I love the lightness it holds. I'm not trying to accomplish anything. It is non-productive time and meant solely for the purpose of spending time together and hearing my son talk, if he wants to.

Usually on those Tuesdays, he shares with me more than he does during the remainder of the week. Because we arrive at it from a place of ease, he feels free to discuss the mundane and sometimes the significant, with me. I have to remind myself to be quiet, to listen, to let him have the space to allow this time to be whatever he wants it to be.

It's my natural tendency to ask prying questions, to be curious about his feelings, hopes, plans, and goals. However, I am able to understand more when I listen and let him lead on our conversations. Even if it is about things that I don't care about, I love to hear him talk.

Yesterday's conversation was about how an airplane engine works and how the steering mechanisms control the actions of the plane. I had no idea what he was talking about, but I listened attentively and nodded. I smiled and invited him to share more.

I know these kind of Tuesdays will soon be gone. For now, I can sit in the sunshine and listen to my teenager explain how an airplane works. I can be in awe of all he is learning and becoming in this moment. I can take joy knowing I fostered a small piece of this learning. I sing praises to God for how he is shaping my son. I can be reminded of the loveliness of this sweet moment of connection. I can be grateful and thank God for Tuesdays.

Think
How can you find a special opportunity to connect with your child on their terms?

"Why, you do not even know what will happen tomorrow. What is your life? You are a mist that appears for a little while and then vanishes." James 4:14

Legacy is created in the life we are designing right now in the ordinary moments.

Recently my father passed away. Being the writer in the family, I was asked to write his obituary. It was hard to sum up an entire life in 500 words or less. My dad fathered nine children and left behind a vast remembrance of family. He was a small-town doctor lavishing care on everyone he met. He had an amazing legacy to share.

As a kid, I can remember going to restaurants and having entire families come to our table with tears in their eyes and share stories about how my dad saved their life. Farmers would show up asking him for his advice about their ailments. Amish families in our community would beam with happiness when we visited their homes, welcoming him like a celebrity. He cared for everyone crossing his path, whether they could pay him or not.

My dad refused to visit anyone without taking a gift. It was always his tradition to take along a token of kindness. I can remember offering hams, loaves of bread, pineapples, chocolates, you name it. I didn't understand it as a kid, but as an adult I get it. His generous way of never showing up empty-handed was a lovely tradition.

My dad could not go anywhere in town without someone calling out his name or thanking him for his most recent thing he did. He left a trail of love and gratitude in his wake. His compassion for everyone went before him and he lavishly doled it out.

My dad wasn't perfect and he had his faults just as I do. Still, I'm so grateful for the sweet memories and lessons he taught me. He instilled in me a passion for gardening and growing things. He wanted his children to know what an adventure cooking could be and took cooking as a family seriously. He was insistent on constantly reading and improving his mind. He loved learning. Even at ninety years old, he was still studying and learning about European history, the French language, and the art of making bread.

Every day we have the opportunity to share a legacy, both in small ways and big ways. My daily actions are my opportunity to share my legacy with my own family and with people who cross my path. Our children see how we are living our legacy with the priorities we set, how we use our time, and how we care for others. Our actions are showing them our hearts.

My hope is to find ways to let my family know how much they are loved by God. My desire is for my family to see me as fully present to them and their days. The simple act of giving my family my full attention and seeing them right where they are, might be the best gift I can give them today.

God gives us only a whisper of time here on earth. Use this gift to bestow on your kids your light and your love, as well as opportunities to demonstrate this in meaningful ways. The days we have with our loved ones will not last forever.

Today, give your child the gift of being with them fully and hearing who they are. Seeing our kids deeply and loving them right where they are is exactly how God loves us. He meets us where we are and loves us there, perfectly. We don't have to earn it and we don't have to perform for it. He loves us entirely. Let your kids see this kind of love at work today, for your legacy tomorrow.

Think
What can you do today to share your family legacy?

Pockets of Rest

"Then, because so many people were coming and going that they did not even have a chance to eat, he said to them, 'Come with me by yourselves to a quiet place and get some rest.'" Mark 6:31

Today is the kind of day where I seek pockets of rest.

My Aunt Betty was a hard scrabble Scottish lady who knew how to work hard and rest hard. She was excellent at modeling the idea of "pockets of rest" in the day. As a child, I remember working by her side doing dishes, cleaning up the kitchen, and polishing things. After a solid time of work, she would say, "Now, let's have a cup of tea." We would then put the tea kettle on and sit down and have a lovely break including tea and Scottish shortbread. It felt luxurious and delightful to have a tea party right in the middle of our labor.

Weaving rest into our everyday rhythms is vital for home-schooling. Shifting my mindset to understand rest is a natural part of working hard shows me it doesn't have to be all or nothing. We can do homeschooling in a kinder, gentler way by making renewal a part of our days.

Start with what a pocket of rest might look like for you.

For me, I like sitting outside. I find renewal in mid-day walks, getting away from my computer or the desk to do some dinner prep, or perhaps a nap. Sometimes, it's watching an inspirational video or listening to soul-enriching music while I clean out the fridge. Perhaps its having a cup of tea and something nourishing like my Aunt Betty did. Figure out what your pockets of rest look like for renewing your body, mind and spirit throughout the day.

Encourage your homeschooling student to think about pockets of rest too. Invite them to get a change of scenery by having a hot cocoa and study time in a local coffee shop with a friend. Pockets of rest might mean planning a get together with friends to celebrate a hard week of work. It might be taking a walk together or going to the gym. Encourage your student to set intentional rest as part of the patterns of their days.

By modeling for your child how to care for yourself well, you are giving them a glimpse of what it looks like to live well. Homeschooling is hard work and can feel like endless drudgery. Show your student that taking time for little breaks and self-care helps us renew as we go.

One day your child will no longer be at home. Far too soon, they will be living on their own, developing their own schedule and habits. They will be creating their own patterns of work, play, rest, and renewal. Help them to figure out now what helps them renew and rest as they work hard. Help them to understand everyone needs breaks to be their best.

Pockets of rest sprinkled throughout your day can be life-giving. Model for your family the idea that rest along the way gives us fuel for the long-term journey of homeschooling.

Think
How can you find pockets of rest in your day?

Coming Alive

"I know that there is nothing better for people than to be happy and to do good while they live. That each of them may eat and drink and find satisfaction in all their toil—this is the gift of God." Ecclesiastes 3:12-13

Good health isn't a place we arrive. As much as I don't like it, taking good care of ourselves is an ongoing journey.

Lately I have been working on figuring out which tiny disciplines fuel me best. I look at my older family members and it motivates me to take better care of myself. My mother smoked for a long time. She had a heart condition and she did not like to exercise if she could help it.

However, she did do a couple things well. She loved to drink water all day. Another habit she did well was to eat loads of vegetables. She loved salads and greens and literally any vegetable she could find. Even with a heart condition, high blood pressure, and being moderately overweight she was able to live well and with fairly good health for most of her remaining years.

For me personally, I want to take my family health lessons to heart and see how I can improve on them. I have adopted my mom's water and vegetable habits as much as I can. I make it a goal to move daily with purpose. To keep this sustainable, movement doesn't need to be an intense style of working out. This could be stretching or taking a walk around the block.

For overall wellness, I think about what helps me feel most alive. I love spending time in nature and taking care of things. I like to water plants, grow things, and watch as things change over time. It gives me joy to see some tiny seed I have miraculously encouraged to become a thriving plant. Also, writing down my thoughts fuels me with a sense of purpose. Sometimes it is writing down my mistakes or where I have fallen short. It could also be prayers to Christ about what gratitude, where I'm struggling, or where I need more guidance. Talking honestly with Christ on a daily basis makes me feel whole.

In homeschooling, my ambition is to provide my child with equipping not only in academics, but in how to live a healthy life. As I seek out the things that help me feel my best, my aim is to encourage my child to do the same. Ultimately, I am preparing my child for when they are no longer under my roof. Whether they go to college, move out, go into mission work, or whatever is next for them, they need to know in detail how to feel their best. The habits they are developing now will be their foundation.

As parents, we can foster wisdom in this area in the example we set. We can model self-care for ourselves and our families. We can invite them to gain clarity on discovering their best selves. We can set the tone for our family to discover vibrant ways to come alive daily.

Think
How can you foster life-giving habits for your family?

Sing

"Sing to the Lord, praise his name; proclaim his salvation day after day." Psalm 96:2

Singing changes me.

If I remember to sing, it's like changing the channel on my mood. Believe me, I'm no singer. Truly, I am not. I remember in one ambitious moment, I signed up to be in our church's Christmas cantata choir. I loved the excuse to sing constantly, even though I'm sure the choir leader wished they had been more selective in their participants.

Besides the regular rehearsals, I practiced every moment I could. I would sing in my car, in the mirror, and while making dinner. When it came time for the actual performance, I was so excited to share the wonder of the music. What I didn't expect is how bored the audience would be. With blank stares, they looked as though they couldn't wait for us to stop.

I learned two things from the singing experience. First, if you are in church, it's important to let your face find out about it. Second, singing changes you. It doesn't matter how gifted you are, you become happier and more grateful by the pure act of making music with your voice. The tunes shared out loud brought a lightness to my heart.

I'm convinced this is because singing requires you to pour out. You cannot pour out what is not there. When you are singing, it is an act of worship, gratitude, and joy. It has to come from somewhere inside of you, even if you have to search the deep recesses of your heart to find it.

Singing requires you to be in the moment. You can't think about tomorrow's worries or yesterday's disappointments. You have to be right where you are, considering the sounds and the words of your song. It requires you to stay present and focused on the goodness right here. It stops the self-indulgent woes. Moving away from tragic thinking, it forces us to find joy. The full press of negativity is put back in the proper place.

I recently read the encouragement, "When in doubt, sing." This is perfect advice. When you find yourself struggling, worried, or scared, try singing. It doesn't have to be lofty church hymns, although I love sacred music. It can be simply humming a tune if you don't know the words. See how the pouring out of sound relaxes you, comforts you, and takes you to a different place.

Every day we have a choice. We can worry, we can be critical, and we can complain. Or, we can sing. The act of making a joyful noise changes my mind and my day. When our kids see us singing in the midst of difficult times, they will see an example of light.

It shows them that even though things are hard, we can still sing. Let your songs inspire a praise-filled heart for your family today.

Think
How can you use music as an act of worship to fuel your heart today?

Listening to Your Life

"... We do not know what to do, but our eyes are on you." 2 Chronicles 20:12

Keep telling yourself, "I can. I can. I can."

Kathy, my fitness class leader, filters through my exercise class as I attempt to do what feels like 100 pushups. I'm probably doing only ten. Or five. With her words and presence, she talks me into doing things I can't believe I actually do. She reminds each of us to tell ourselves, "I can."

What's funny is, I believe her. For an hour straight, Kathy speaks to the group with words of affirmation such as, "You are so strong. You got this. You are more powerful than you know." When I'm done, I'm amazed at what I have accomplished. I listened to Kathy. I didn't listen to the other voices that said, "You are tired. This is hard. Quit. Give up."

When Kathy the trainer pours positive things over me, I cannot help but listen. It feels like I'm hearing these encouraging thoughts for the first time. I want to believe the positive things. I want goodness to cover my heart and mind.

In homeschooling, we can listen to the voices saying we have no business doing this. We can choose to take in the negative thoughts telling us we aren't smart enough or talented enough. Or, we can choose to listen to the higher, Christ-like words of grace and love. We can listen to thoughts of goodness as our guide.

Instead of *"I can't do this,"* we shift to, *"I can do all things through Christ."*

Instead of *"This is too hard for me,"* we can move to, *"Christ is in me and He has overcome the world."*

Instead of *"I don't know how to do this,"* we can say, *"I have no idea what to do, but my eyes are on You Lord."*

Negative self-talk serves no one. When I deeply listen to how I speak to myself, I sometimes use words I wouldn't even say to my dog. I want better than that for myself. Our words are so powerful. Use yours to equip yourself and others. I am learning to be intentional about surrounding myself with people who remind me who I am in Christ. I long to use my words to build up, inspire, and encourage others. I want to be water and life to myself and those who surround me.

Practice saying kind things to your heart, as a way to express the love our Creator first poured out. Tell yourself, *"I can. I am loved. Christ is with me. Now let's go conquer the day."* Let your words remind you of the love that is already there. Christ didn't die for us so that we would be condemned to negativity. He died so that we could live a life full of goodness. Tell yourself and others those life-giving, loving words today.

Think
Where do you most need to speak words of loving kindness today?

```
┌─────────────────────────────────────────┐
│                                           │
│         Designing the Future You          │
│                                           │
└─────────────────────────────────────────┘
```

"...being confident of this, that he who began a good work in you will carry it on to completion until the day of Christ Jesus." Philippians 1:6

What will your life look like in ten years?

It's hard to imagine 10 days from now, let alone 10 years. However, I was recently listening to a speaker that invited guests to consider the "ten years from now" notion. She asked the audience if they would be happy if their life were to remain exactly the same, ten years from now.

When put in those terms, it inspired me to get serious about changing things. For me, it's not that I wasn't happy with my life. I genuinely liked what I was doing. But if I were thinking of my future life design, I knew there were some longings in my heart to consider. I decided it was time to get after some of the hopes and dreams still in my heart.

Homeschooling is a commitment. I definitely sidelined some ambitions and projects until I felt I had more mental bandwidth. Yet I could appreciate things were progressing in our homeschool life to reveal my child needed me a little bit less each year. Hopefully, this same experience will be true for you in your homeschool environment.

With fresh inspiration, I began to consider some ideas for life after homeschool. Would I return to the workforce? Start a business? Get more involved with church, service, hobbies, or passions? Where would I like to see myself after your home-schooling journey is over? I began to consider what small steps I could begin to "try on" the next season ahead.

Just as I did when I was designing our homeschool year, I started with passions. This time I was looking at my own passions to see where I wanted to focus my energies. I knew I wanted to get back into writing and I treasured pouring into students. With that in mind, I looked for small ways to begin to do more writing. Sometimes this meant getting up earlier or squeezing fifteen minutes of writing into my lunch breaks. I also started paying more attention to service opportunities with tutoring and mentoring outside of my homeschooling communities to broaden my environment.

One of the things that I missed most during our home-school years was being able to have lunch with friends. For me, I found it disruptive and counterproductive if I left the house in the middle of the homeschool day. In the next season, I wanted to be intentional about making more time for friends and loved ones. This meant I needed to be intentional about spending time with loved ones where I could now. Previously, I felt I didn't have time to join any additional activities but now had more time for women's ministry events, books clubs and other engaging ways to connect with friends.

In truth, it's hard to know what my life would be like ten years from now. I know I have missed my friends and some of my passions minimized in the homeschooling season. As I was considering the homestretch, I wanted to model for my son a parent who also pursued their own hopes and dreams. While my student was preparing for life beyond homeschooling, I needed to be as intentional about preparing for my life beyond homeschooling, too.

<u>Think</u>
What will life look like for you after homeschooling? What are small ways you can begin to try those ideas on now?

Waking Up

"Arise, shine, for your light has come, and the glory of
the Lord rises upon you." Isaiah 60:1

"What is that noise?" a friend asked me recently while talking on
the phone.

It was a bright spring day and the birds were out in full
force, chirping happily in the sunshine. It was a gorgeous
cacophony of sounds. Until my friend pointed it out, I hadn't
noticed it at. all. I was caught up in doing, not noticing the
wonder serenading my morning.

I find it's easy to fall asleep in my routines. If I'm not careful, I can hurriedly shove lunch in my face, while I try to catch
up on emails and texts. I can rush through making dinner for
my family and distractedly clean up afterwards, not really
seeing people's faces or noticing anyone's feelings. My default
setting on the day can look like autopilot if I'm not
intentional.

I can also choose to wake up. At lunchtime, I can notice
how perfect the avocado is as I spread it out on my favorite
toast. I can take some extra time to add some fresh greens and
make it look like a chef's creation with a drizzle of olive oil

and a crank of sea salt. I can take a moment to savor. It doesn't have to be a long time, maybe ten or fifteen minutes. I can take time to taste and see and be grateful.

I can sit down before my meal and take a deep breath. I can pray with a simple, "Thank you God." I can notice the creaminess of the avocado texture contrasting with the brightness of the greens and crunch of the toast. I can chew slowly instead of shoving food down. I can hydrate well with a tall glass of water. I can make this moment about noticing, self-care, and gratitude.

Instead of mindlessly asking my family how their day was, I can stop what I'm doing and look them in the eye. I can ask them something authentic, "What was the best thing that happened today?" Or I can tell them a funny story that I know they would love. I can be present to all of it instead of multi-tasking through dinner preparations, reading the mail, and pretend conversations in which I'm not really there.

I don't want to miss these little things. I know it's these ordinary, everyday, stuff-of-life moments I will look back on and remember. Soon I will long for the days when my family was all here together under one roof, when life was full and abundant with activities and school.

I want to savor these things as I go, instead of hurriedly moving on from one task to the next. I don't want to get more done. I want to treasure more and see more. I want to be present to life as it is happening. I want to set the example for my family and invite them to see the beauty in life as it unfolds in every day we are given. I want them to see God in the little things. I want to wake up.

Think
How can you wake up to see more of the beauty in your life?

```
┌─────────────────────────────────┐
│                                 │
│                                 │
│            Move It              │
│                                 │
└─────────────────────────────────┘
```

"For physical training is of some value, but godliness has value for all things, holding promise for both the present life and the life to come." 1 Timothy 4:8

No matter what is happening in the day, I always feel better when I move my body.

It doesn't have to be a lot of movement, sometimes it's only a quick walk around the neighborhood. Other times it's a longer, intense workout. Sometimes, I like something more peaceful, like stretching and yoga. The point is to move.

Some days I feel like I've met my limit on the inside. I'm maxed out emotionally or mentally. When I remember to get outside, to move my body, and focus on my breath, it changes something in my head. I don't know if it's the mere act of separating myself from the geography of home or if it's the physical change happening as a result. I am better when I move.

For some days, I don't have time for a real workout. At those times, I do jumping jacks while I wait for my toast or I do ten pushups while I'm waiting for water to boil. The little pockets of movement and exercise may not be huge, but they are something. Over the course of the day, those five-minute bursts of exercise can equal thirty minutes or more when you put them together.

Look for sneaky ways to get more movement in your days. Park as far away as you can away from the grocery store entrance. Do squats when you are put on hold on the phone. Work standing up if you can throughout the day. Anytime you have to wait for something, whether it's toast, a kettle, or a child, throw in some jumping jacks, pushups, lunges, or sit-ups. Do what you can in the time you have. Just move.

If you can, encourage your student to take a walk with you. They may roll their eyes or say they don't have time to do it. Still, if they have been sitting at their desk for too long, encourage them to take a quick walk around the block with you. Depending on your student, you could use the time to be productive by quizzing them on flashcards as you walk. Other times, this may be a chance not to talk about school and let them share what is on their heart. I tried to be open to letting my child guide our time together.

The best "walk talks" were when I shut up and made space for my son to share his thoughts. I had to remind myself to let the walk be just a walk and a chance to connect with my child without the pressure of performance, too.

My encouragement is to make movement a priority. Set the example for your family that movement is a habit. It could be walks, weight training, gardening, or jumping jacks while you wait for the toast. Encourage your student and your family to make movement a regular part of each day.

Impress upon your student that moving your body in a healthy way is equally as important a habit as study skills and academics. Model how movement helps everyone de-stress and take care of bodies and minds.

<u>Think</u>
How can you set the example to move with purpose during the day?

In Search of Fun

"Nehemiah said, "Go and enjoy choice food and sweet drinks, and send some to those who have nothing prepared. This day is holy to our Lord. Do not grieve, for the joy of the Lord is your strength." Nehemiah 8:10

Can homeschooling be fun?

After all, this is serious business. We debate important ideas, pursue rigorous academics, and think deep thoughts. Since my son's whole future is depending on homeschooling, my tendency is to create intense pressure on myself for all of it. If I'm not careful, I can take out all the fun.

There is fun to be found in homeschooling, but it starts as an inside job. If your heart and mind are in a bad place, there is no amount dressing up your attitude that will help things become more fun. Homeschooling is as fun as you decide for it to be. For me, that means I need to spend time with Christ in prayer and devotion to begin the day. When my heart is aligned with His, I give myself the best chance to experience joy.

To be real, I'm not always "joy-filled," but I can seek His

face for help to find it. Some days are better than others and I have to trust that working through difficult emotions will ultimately be a blessing. There is joy to be found, even when it's hard.

Fun can be an outside job, too. When I was tutoring students, I made it a point to wear bright colors. I did this for two reasons: to boost my mood and also to be physically bright for the kids. I think fun needs to start by putting something on that makes you feel positive. For me, not wearing workout clothes all day is helpful. Dressing as if I were going to a fun outing somewhere (even if I'm not) makes me feel happier.

There is no judgement if wearing yoga clothes or pajamas all day is fun for you. I know how you look also dictates how you feel. If I feel clean and pulled together with a squirt of perfume and some bright lipstick, I feel fun. I feel positive, energized. I look good and I feel good. When I am orderly in my physical body, I am ready for joy.

With my daily tasks, I can choose things that speak joy in my environment. If it's a rainy Tuesday and I'm in a terrible mood, praise and worship music can uplift my heart. Perhaps I'll put something delicious in the slow cooker to make the house smell amazing. I might light a candle to remind me to enjoy the moment. I can journal scriptures and personalize them to remind me how dearly loved, valuable, and forgiven I am in Christ. I can sprinkle joy everywhere into my day.

Lastly, I consider my "joy filter" with what I allow into my mind on a daily basis. Social media and the daily news send me down the rabbit hole of depression. I am learning to limit this influence. If I screen my calls, voicemail, doorbell, and mail, it makes sense I would do the same with social media and news. In order to leverage our lives for fun, we have to be strategic about what we allow into our circle of influence.

I am intentional about planning and designing the school year for my student. I am focused when I think about caring for my family. If those are both true, I can also be strategic about cultivating happiness and joy. Every day will not be like heaven, but I can choose joy. Making small simple choices in our everyday lives allows us to see more of the good stuff at work. We serve a God who wants us to experience abundant love and abundant fun in our homeschooling season.

Think
How can you design your day to choose joy?

Radical

"The thief comes only to steal and kill and destroy; I have come that they may have life, and have it to the full." John 10:10

I've always wanted to learn to surf.

Partly I like the idea because it seems ridiculous yet amazing at the same time. Lately, little nudges have been showing up on my path. Magazine articles dedicated to an issue on fitness for surfing speak to me. Friends mention they are heading to the ocean for the weekend and I sense a tug of longing. When scanning the catalogs in the mail, my heart resonates with the beautiful ocean images featuring strong, vibrant women surfing the ocean curls.

Surfing is something I always tell myself, "Someday I'm going to learn to surf." It's the dream which lives way far off in the distance and stays there. There are a million reasons why I haven't done anything about this surf dream. The excuses range from everything like, "I'm too old" or "It's too expensive" or "That seems self-indulgent." The dream dies before it even begins.

For me, surfing represents risk. It represents doing something physically challenging completely outside of my comfort zone. Wearing a swimsuit in public is terrifying enough by itself. Putting myself out there physically and risking looking bad or failing completely is scary. Surfing means being in a place where I have no idea what I'm doing.

I keep thinking of all the reasons why surfing is a bad idea. I could get caught in a rip current. There might be sharks. I'm not sure I can physically get up on a surfboard. The weather might be terrible. I could get stung by a jellyfish. I could get terribly sunburned. I might end up hating surfing after all this time of dreaming about it.

I can only think of one good reason why I should surf: to ride a wave.

Lately, I have come to a point in life where I want to dream. I'm not getting any younger. I'm ready to take small steps toward beginning this dream. I'm tired of waiting and saying no to myself. I'm tired of talking myself out of risks because it's easier and more comfortable not to try.

I want to be the kind of person who has adventures, not the person who only reads about them. I want to be the kind of person who lives a full and beautiful life for God. Scripture says in John 10:10 (NIV), *"The thief comes to steal, kill and destroy; I have come that they may have life and have it in abundance."*

I want to live an abundant life. I think Christ wants us to have an abundant life, too, full of joys, adventures, hopes, and dreams. Much of what I do, day in and day out, is about service to family, my church, my community. I believe it is an awesome calling and I love it completely. However, Jesus inspired hopes and dreams in our hearts for a reason. He places them in our heart so we can see more of Him in this world. He is for us. He encourages us to consider this abundance not only for our families, but for ourselves, too.

What is your thing? What is the thing you have always dreamed about and wondered what it might be like to experience? God gave us hearts for abundance and dreams. Living out our faith is about loving God and worshipping Him with our actions. Like homeschooling, boldly living out the desires of our heart can also be an act of faithful worship.

<u>Think</u>
What is a dream lurking in your heart? What is one small step you can take to pursue it today?

```
┌─────────────────────────────────────────┐
│                                           │
│                                           │
│                 Refresh                   │
│                                           │
└─────────────────────────────────────────┘
```

"See, I am doing a new thing! Now it springs up; do you not perceive it? I am making a way in the wilderness and streams in the wasteland." Isaiah 43:19

Every summer, I love to re-read a classic devotional book called, *Streams in the Desert*[1] by L. B. Cowman. Written originally in 1925, it has a wise, old-school feel. The name of the book originates from the idea of refreshment in Christ and scriptures of Living Waters. After a hard year of homeschooling, this resource always gives offers much needed encouragement.

When I read Isaiah 43:19 with the images of fresh water in the wilderness, it reminds me God wants to do something refreshing in our family and in our homeschool. However, if I keep pressing on with plans and busy-ness, I may never stop to see it. The summer season offers the chance to see something fresh at work in our family. It allows me to stop, to see, to hear, and to receive His guidance for the new thing He wants to inspire in the season ahead.

During the school year, I long for the idea of summer. I long for unscheduled and unstructured days. I dream of the carefree mornings and afternoons, free from zooming in the car from activity to activity. Instead, I treasure summer days filled with our favorite things like hikes in the park, stargazing, board games, and eating outside in the golden light.

During the summer, I long for the structure and order of the school day. I'm struggling to relax into knowing school will return soon enough. Rest is about trust. It's trusting it's okay to put all of the busy-ness aside and goof off for a while.

This summer my hope is to goof off. I want to set aside the constant doing for a little while. We have to wait and rest in Him. We have to pause and listen. We have to rest before journeying ahead. We have to be still enough to be ready for the new thing God is doing. We have to embrace the quiet so we have fresh eyes to see the streams in the desert.

I think about what my child needs most this summer. I go to the closet and I get out our favorite board games -- Settlers of Catan, Scrabble Apples, and Uno. I set up a puzzle we have been longing to do. I put out some books we have been saving to read in a slower season, which are purely fun. I'm practicing goofing off by creating an ecosystem of goodness, ready for us to enjoy.

My hope is to rest in Him. I wait with a hopeful heart for the new thing God will do in our family this year. I set aside my ruminations in favor of noticing this gorgeous moment of summer. I can't wait to see what streams in the desert our loving Father will create in our lives this year. I surrender my spirit so I will be ready for the fresh thing He is doing in our family. I will trust and rest in Him.

Think
How can you refresh during the summer season?

6

Finishing Strong
CHAPTER SIX

Ideas and equipping for wrapping up your homeschool season.

"I have fought the good fight, I have finished the race, I kept the faith." 2 Timothy 4:7

Finishing Strong

"I have fought the good fight, I have finished the race, I kept the faith." 2 Timothy 4:7

The end of the year is in sight and all I can think about is summer.

Exactly when high-level motivation needs to kick in, our family is running out of steam. How do we dig deep to stay motivated to finish the school year strong?

Preparing for year-end finals and projects can be overwhelming. To help streamline the final stretch, I encouraged my son to consider what he needed to focus on for today only. We made it a priority to think about the "big three" each day - - what are the three things he needed to do today? By declaring his key three, it helped start the day with the most important things first.

Another idea for finishing strong is to think fun. Invite your student to think of creative and fun ways to mix up their school and final preparation time. Perhaps inviting a friend to study with them will help them stay motivated. Working in a coffee shop might give them a needed change of geography. Challenge them to work for a solid hour and then take a break with their favorite snack or activity. Any motivation you can add in whether it's food, friends, or fun, can go a long way to helping them work through to the end.

It's tempting to think "all or nothing" about school. As our family wraps up the academics, I'm thinking about small things to keep everyone on track. My son struggles the most with how to schedule all of the end of year planning. Because he was open to coaching, I encouraged to think about his final prep in bite-sized pieces for the final weeks.

Breaking things down to small increments feels like simple advice, but teens sometimes need a refresher on the basics of planning. I encouraged my son to begin with the end and work backwards. I asked him to mark the end dates then work back to present day, thinking through how much time he can dedicate to the priorities. I encouraged him to put it somewhere he could see it and reference it often -- on a large wall calendar, a white board, or even a simple piece of paper.

From the big picture, I encouraged my son to think about each week. Sometimes mapping things out visually on paper or a whiteboard shows what it looks like to break it down. This helped my son to see he only needed to focus on bite-sized pieces of time instead of an infinite, never-ending study session.

As the school year wraps up, the details and deadlines can be overwhelming. We can be tossed about by our emotions, fears, and anxiety. Invite God to order your day. Pray with your child to invite our heavenly Father to direct their steps to finish the year strong. Model for your child to see when life becomes stressful, we can lean on the Father's love to see us through.

Think
How can you encourage your family to finish the year strong?

Missing It

"I will remember the deeds of the Lord; yes, I will remember your miracles of long ago. I will consider all your works and meditate on all your mighty deeds." Psalm 77: 11-12

This is my son's senior year and I feel like I'm missing it.

There is a strain in my voice when he leaves each morning with the send-off words: "Be careful!" and "I love you!" and "Make good choices!" The truth is, I do feel desperate. Nothing is comforting and there is a constant voice in my head keeps screeching, "YOU SHOULD BE ENJOYING THIS MOMENT!"

All of it feels hard. Even when I plan memorable things, it feels forced. Because I am putting so much pressure and weight on everything, I cannot enjoy anything.

Some days are better than others. Some days we decorate the house for the holidays and my son and I catch eyes with our inside jokes. Some days my son comes home from his classes and I ask if he wants biscuits his favorite way with butter and jam. I get a nod and a smile from him and it's as if we are speaking our own secret language.

There are the other sort of days when he doesn't want to speak to me at all. He asks me to stop hovering and closes his door. He craves distance and I can tell he's embarrassed to have a parent near him and his friends. While he works at his desk, I stop to say hello and I know he can't wait for me to leave.

I don't understand why this is so hard. I raised my kid to be kind, embrace his faith, and explore the vast knowledge of life and virtue. I trained him to go out into the world and be the best version of himself. Now I am suddenly surprised when he does. This is the moment I have been designing all of his growing up years to embrace.

Still, I keep looking for ways not to miss it, desperately trying to be here now. I remind myself to stop, to notice the sights and smells, and to pause to remember there will never be a season like this one. In truth, each day and season we are given will never be the same as another. It's all part of the life experience for everyone, no matter the season. The place where we are in today will always be different from where we were even a moment before.

My hope is to find a way to draw it all in. I let go of lofty and worldly expectations of what it needs to be. I give myself grace to know I can't stop time. I can only treasure the moment I have before me. I look to this day, gathering in each moment, season by season.

Think
How can you be present to this day?

Strawberry Season

"Therefore, as God's chosen people, holy and dearly loved, clothe yourself in compassion, kindness, humility, gentleness and patience." Colossians 3:12

As soon as we start to see pop-up curbside stands for strawberries, I can't help but smile. Strawberry season means the school year is almost over. With lighter days on the way, it feels as though we've been given permission to take a deep breath and relax.

At the end of the school year, usually around Mother's Day, we make strawberry jam as our year-end tradition. My mom and I would buy huge flats of strawberries and spend afternoons together making jam and celebrating summer's arrival. Typically, in the background, we would hear shouts from rowdy boys playing board games or having water balloon fights for an end of year get-together.

God was a genius when He designed the seasons to allow natural, renewing rhythms of working hard at school for a time and then working hard at playing for a time. At the end of every school year, we celebrate our traditions for wrapping up the year. These traditions are our way to take stock of what we have learned, have some fun, and put the school year to rest.

First, there was a day we would spend deep cleaning the school room. We would go back over old papers, presentations, projects, and photos. These would be three-hole punched or filed away in the school binder to capture the year's highlights. As well, we would always have year-end park gatherings with friends to celebrate the year and kick off the summer season.

My favorite ritual was to head to my small hometown in Michigan after the school year was complete. We would spend a week visiting family and enjoying the wide-open spaces of vast fields at my sister's horse farm. The days started and ended with no agenda, checklists, or plans of any sort. We loved having a week of unscheduled days simply to have breakfast, go for long walks, and enjoy family with no time constraints and requirements.

As the school year winds down, think about how you can celebrate the year and take stock of all that your family experienced. Include your child in the planning and invite them to think of some meaningful activities. Some families would head to the beach or the mountains. Others would go camping or take road trips. For other friends, they vowed to stay in their pajamas for a week straight and do nothing but play games, rest, read, and head to local parks.

Design some beautiful rituals reflecting your family's style as you close out the year. Consider weaving in extended family or friends who were supportive of you and your year. Expressing gratitude to others for their encouragement and fellowship is also a vital part of commemorating the year.

Taking time to celebrate your school year with intention is equally as important as planning your school year well. By taking time to commemorate God's provision and kindness for the year, you are creating sweet memories as a family. Before summer rushes in, pause with your family to reflect and remember God's faithfulness.

Think
How will you celebrate the school year's end?

God Academics

"...but test them all; hold on to what is good." 1 Thessalonians 5:21

As our family wraps up the school year, I like to take stock.

I ask my son questions like, "What worked well this year?" and "What didn't work well this year?" We discuss his "take-aways" or the things he was most proud of during the school year. More important than achievements or failures, the better question might be, "What has God taught us this year?"

When I look at this question, I typically think about spiritual disciplines. My default is to make my mental list of tangible achievements. Things like participating in a church small group weekly, spending time in prayer and the Word daily. Our family attended church on a mostly regular basis and did our best to apply the sermons to our lives. All of that feels simply like God productivity to me.

More than learning about God, I looked deeper and ask, "How am I different this year after spending time with Christ?"

When I consider this authentic question, I see how God has been nudging me forward. Christ is moving me to release control over my child and his future. I am starting to deeply and fully appreciate God's plans as always better and higher. Christ is revealing how pauses and spaces in our days are where He is able to show up. The word "no" has become a complete sentence. Lastly, God in His goodness is showing me not to get ahead of Him.

I can't say that I'm all the way there yet. There are days when I take back trying to control or micromanage things. Still God, in His kind mercy, shows me how much better things can be when I release it to Him.

When I allow Him to move first, it gives my child space to grow. He develops confidence or he makes a mistake and learns. His character becomes stronger because he has had to figure it out or muddle through. He learns what it's like to persevere. For me, I free up my anxious thoughts and worried ruminations. This gives me time to do more of what I love such as work, cook, volunteer, garden, journal, or write. When I let go of the meddling, I am freed up to be more of the person God intended me to be.

As you wrap up the year, ask your student, "What has God taught you this year?" or even better yet, "How are you different as a result of spending time with Christ?" Not only is this a wonderful question for our kids, it is a good one for ourselves, too. As Christ followers, every school year is the opportunity to continue to walk deeper in the waters of our faith. We serve a personal God, who never leaves us as we are. He loves us enough to keep growing us day by day, year by year.

Think
How are you different as a result of spending time with Christ this year?

Yes, Homeschoolers Do Go to Prom

"See what great love the Father has lavished on us, that we should be called children of God! And that is what we are!" 1 John 3:1

Unlike unicorns and Big Foot, homeschool proms do exist and I have pictures to prove it. Most people falsely assume homeschoolers will never experience prom. Most of the homeschoolers I know have every opportunity to go to prom or make their own.

Grocery store clerks with worried faces have questioned me with deep concern if my child would ever go to prom. Family members would take me aside at special gatherings to inquire why I would homeschool and miss out on such valuable milestone experiences like homecoming dances and prom. The truth is most homeschoolers do have the chance to enjoy prom.

I get it. Prom felt like an essential rite of passage for the high school experience.

Regardless of whether you think prom is important or prom carries too much cost and pressure, there are proms available for homeschoolers.

As for my son, he and his friends organized a group of guys to go to the area homeschooling prom their junior year. They made it a challenge for each other to go as a group and agreed they would make it a fun time. My son is not the "I love prom" sort, so it took him a long time to come around to deciding to go. He chose to have low expectations and to think of it as a fun evening out.

Based on the pictures of his prom night, the prom looked like a more stylish experience than many weddings. He and his friends danced with other girls who didn't have dates. They loved cutting up on the dance floor and created some fun memories. The stories he told later made my stomach hurt from laughing so hard at their dancing antics and innocent mischief.

Prom didn't change his life. He had a good time, he made some memories and then it was over. It was one night and it was a fun one. But it wasn't his defining moment.

Other homeschooling friends have organized their own version of proms that matched their style. Some were line dancing events with a "caller" to tell dancers what to do. Some were more etiquette-focused with a cultural event afterwards. Others were exactly like a traditional prom. Some even felt like an over-the-top wedding with candy buffets, prop-filled photo booths and glamorous gazebos. I assure you, if you want a certain style of prom, it is available. Or if it isn't in your area, you and a group of friends can create one in your own taste.

God is so creative in the way homeschoolers enjoy life. They can make it their own and without pressure from others to have to match what everyone else is doing. We serve a personal God who loves us and cares for us personally. We get to share this same kind of lavish love with our kids to do things in their own way.

<u>Think</u>
What are your family's thoughts around prom? How will you handle questions about prom?

"Since we live by the Spirit, let us keep in step with the Spirit." Galatians 5:25

Summer means the three Rs in our family. Or as I like to call it, "school light."

Since learning is an ecosystem, it doesn't have to stop once the calendar shows a certain date. After the steady rhythm of homeschooling, our family struggled in the summers without any form of structure at all. With that in mind, we created the idea of "school light" for summers.

To be clear, we did not do school all summer long. We took plenty of long vacations or breaks from school both during the school year and in the summer. But a common thread for an ordinary summer meant a little reading, a little writing, and a little bit of math. Each summer looked different in every season according to my child's age, abilities, and interests.

Some summers it meant reading certain books to prepare for the upcoming year. The year my student studied US History, he read several biographies and stories in the American history theme. There were summers when my child spent time working on standardized testing practices in math, reading, or writing for the ACT or SAT. There were also summers he read what he wanted, kept a nature journal, or listened to audiobooks.

Truly, my child didn't love that I required him to do the three Rs during the summer. Your child may not love it either. The point is to never stop learning. It doesn't need to be intense or stressful. It needed to simply be. Without it, I noticed my child would become out of sorts, bored and complaining much of the time. Having some sort of focus during the summer helped keep some intention for the day. In the end, this made for an easier transition back into the school year.

Later in high school, we found teachers required him to read books during the summer and to complete summer assignments prior to the school year start. When it came to preparing college essays, college applications, and other tasks during the summer, it was already a habit. As a natural extension of the way we were already operating, a summer focus helped my child stay balanced.

My three Rs may not be a fit for you. My encouragement is to be intentional with your summers. Think about how you can keep a love of learning going even though it may be a slower season. Consider how to continue setting out a nourishing feast of learning. Perhaps it's more involved cooking, baking, artistic projects, field trips, or travel adventures. The most important thing is to keep the learning going.

This advice works for parents, too. During the summer months, I would get together with a group of homeschool parents for a "summer book club." We had more time in the summer for reading and discussions. Typically, we would pick out a book for equipping ourselves as parents or we would select a challenging literature book to dive into and discuss. The accountability of other parents helped me to stay motivated. Our children watch what we do and this was our chance to show them we were equally dedicated to learning.

Whether you take on "school light" or decide to go on a road trip as a family, look for intentional ways to weave a love of learning into your summer. The hope is to create life-long learners who see everything as a chance to increase in knowledge for Him. Summer is a perfect time to savor the feast of ideas with your family.

Think
How can you be intentional with summertime enrichment for yourself and your family?

Relish

"Then you will shine among them like stars in the sky as you hold firmly to the word of life. And then I will be able to boast on the day of Christ that I did not run or labor in vain." Philippians 2: 15-16

You know it's a celebration when the relish jar appears.

Every Fourth of July, like clockwork, we would buy a new jar of relish to use with hotdogs at the backyard cookout. The relish would get used by one brave odd soul who actually liked the vinegary, picklish condiment. Then the relish jar would sit in the fridge for the next year, unused or even considered.

Relish is special. It's a reminder that celebrations are but a brief moment and don't come around very often. We need to enjoy them right now, today. If I can wake up to my days, I can appreciate I will never have this moment again.

I want my homeschool heart to be like relish. I want to truly see I won't always have these days. It's hard to imagine a time in my life when my to-do list won't involve reviewing Latin verbs, planning ahead for college visits, and making sure all of my son's homework is completed weekly. I can't imagine a day without driving the carpool to chemistry lab, piano lessons, or hockey practice.

Yet, I know it's coming. As sure as the relish on the Fourth of July, my homeschooling days are numbered. How do you enjoy the relish, right here, right now, in the midst of the chaos, workload, and stress of a regular day?

Knowing we prepare our kids to launch and leave us, it's still a hard knowing to take. If we have done our work well, they can't wait to discover all that life has for them. We nourish them lovingly, carefully, and with the understanding that it's only a matter of time before they leave and break our hearts.

For me, the relishing starts by being grateful. Even though it is stressful and busy right now, I can have gratitude. What will my child say about these days we have had? Will he remember me yelling at him for not completing his homework or will he remember I made hot cocoa and popcorn for him to enjoy while watching Latin videos?

The homeschooling journey is hard. It requires fortitude, confidence, and trusting in an outcome which may never be seen in this lifetime. But it also requires a bit of relish. It requires that you step outside the ordinary of the everyday and take time to see what is beautiful right now. It reminds you that even a pickled concoction can make it a celebration. If that is true, what can you celebrate today in the midst of it all?

Think
What do you need to celebrate right now in your homeschool?

The Sacred Art of Parenting

"Start children off on the way they should go, and even when they are old they will not turn from it." Proverbs 22:6

If I'm doing my homeschooling job well, I ultimately will be fired.

My brain understands this obvious idea. My heart fights the fact that all this work is done with the goal of my child leaving.

As my teenager prepares to leave for college, his focus changes outward. He is still involved in Bible study, church, and Christian groups, but home is no longer central to his life. He is forging his own path, interests, and pursuits that do not include us or time together.

From other friends I have learned it is pretty normal and typical for teens to begin to sever family ties as they prepare to leave home. Some kids can be downright mean during this season. I can rationalize this as their own emotional preparation for going off on their own. If your child still keeps family central to their life, my encouragement is to be grateful. But if your child is separating from all things at home, know that this is normal, too.

At times this separation hurts me deeply. I never expected my engaging, laid back, and easygoing son to suddenly become aloof and avoiding at times. My son is still a good kid and pursuing lots of neat things. He isn't depressed or running with the wrong crowd. He is busy with work, studies, friends, and social activities. He limits his time with us and chooses to spend his free time on his own or without us. I find this hard, but I know it's what is supposed to happen.

People have told me when kids want to separate from their family, it means they are trying to figure things out on their own. It is our children's way of becoming adults. They need to sort through life on their terms and in their own space. Friends have reassured me if they were once a good and loving kid, in time they will return back to being a good and loving adult.

I want my son to grow up, love God, be independent, honor and respect his family and parents. I want him to also know how to figure things out on his own and to learn to trust his own abilities and judgement. I know this can only come with practice and time. I have to give him the space to test it out.

I know this growing up and leaving process is what is supposed to happen. I am grateful for all the memories and adventures we have had. I wait with a heart full of hope for the young man he is becoming in Christ. I pray God will see him through and the education we worked through together is enough in Him. I know God will be faithful in however things turn out. I trust Him and know this heartbreak is also part of the journey.

Think
What are your thoughts and beliefs about your child's leaving home?

Now What?

"Taste and see that the Lord is good; blessed is the one who takes refuge in him." Psalm 34:8

As my son nears graduation, people keep asking me what I'm going to do with myself.

Having spent the last ten years homeschooling, all I ever thought about was getting to the end. With the end coming soon, every day it becomes more real. The clarity I had when I started homeschooling now feels like the complete opposite feeling for what I'm going to be doing next.

Sometimes I engage in the "mom fantasy" plans of imaging myself going back to the corporate world, working out, lunching with friends, volunteering for causes, and dedicating life to things I have sidelined during the homeschooling season. Then there is the terrifying part of the forthcoming reality where I might be curled in the fetal position and smelling my son's old shirts.

I think about what's next and I can't see it. I fear I will never find anything as meaningful and purposeful as what I'm doing right now. I never imagined how all these years of joy, hardship, suffering, and doing life together through home-schooling changed our family.

No amount of corporate jobs or lunches with friends could ever add up to the soul refining depths homeschooling has given me. Don't get me wrong, it was never easy. Whether I was homeschooling one child or ten children, it would never have been an easy endeavor. But it changed me. It required me to become more of who God intended. It demanded I walk by faith and not by standards the world valued. It challenged me to trust Him even when I couldn't see the end. Just like now.

Here I am almost at the end and again I can't see what is next. I continue the only way I know how, searching for where God is at work and joining Him. I look and listen for His nudges to show me where He wants me to walk, whether it's at a job, volunteering, or taking some time to simply rest. Homeschooling has taught me God will show me where to walk. I have to be willing to wait and look for it.

Instead of fretting about what I'm going to be doing a year from now, I have decided to be present in this moment. I look for where I can help, encourage, and love. If my son doesn't need me in this moment, I have other good things to do like mentoring other homeschool moms and volunteering my time with kids that need someone to come alongside them, too.

Even though this chapter is ending, my ability to pour into others and encourage doesn't end. It simply takes on a new look and feel. It may have a different outfit, but it is still love in the same package.

Think
How can you consider the next season while staying present to life before you?

Not the End

"...being confident of this, that he who began a good work in you will carry it on to completion until the day of Christ Jesus." Philippians 1:6

My mom refused to finish books she loved.

If you love the book, why not finish it? For her, she enjoyed the characters and the story, and in her mind ending it meant they weren't part of her life anymore. They were like friends requiring a permanent good-bye once the story ended. As a result, she couldn't bear finishing good books.

In some ways, homeschooling feels the same way. It's a story and an adventure I'm not sure I want to end. I know not everyone feels this way and when you are knee deep in the struggles, the end can't come soon enough. Truly, the point of homeschooling is to finish. The journey began with the ultimate hope that one day I would celebrate a confident, wise, virtuous, and ready-for-the-world young person. Holding this vision in my heart, my hope rested in my child ready to walk their own path with confidence.

I never thought I would long for it *not* to end. Perhaps it is because homeschooling required so much of me. It demanded my full reliance on God and gave a special purpose to each day. The transformative process felt as if I was truly on an important mission for our family.

Then one day, like today, it's done. I know it's right for it to end. Yet I still wonder if there will be any activity or pursuit as meaningful as raising your children to love the Lord and discover all their education offers?

I think yes and no.

I think there will never be anything quite like living the homeschooling journey with your family. Through all we endured, enjoyed, appreciated, and overcame with God's help, nothing will be like it. However, God won't leave us there. He prepared us not only to learn, but to do His will.

It's like reading the Word: we can't simply read the Word and know about God. We have to be transformed and then put whatever gifts He has called us to use into action. The learning journey is truly beginning. It's time for my child to take it from here, with God's help.

Now that this season is almost complete for me, my desire is to fill it with activity. I want to stay so busy with work, volunteering, and activities to avoid thinking about what is missing. I don't want to notice the giant gaping hole in my days. Yet I know that doesn't honor God.

I walk forward with a hopeful heart into an unknown season without homeschooling. I wait in anticipation to see what God is going to do in this unfamiliar place. I trust God has something new for me ahead. I know I need to wait on Him. I only want it if He's in it.

Think
How do you feel about finishing homeschooling? Where do you need to embrace unknown places in your homeschool season?

Love the Change

"So this is what the Sovereign Lord says: 'See, I lay a stone in Zion, a tested stone, a precious cornerstone for a sure foundation.'" Isaiah 28:16

A recent Pampers diapers ad sweetly features these words, *"Love the Change."* The commercial celebrates how a newborn baby changes everything. Strange sleep patterns, weird smells, unwieldy car seats, and giant loads of tiny laundry piles. It definitely changes everything. Their encouragement was to "love the change."

I'm working on loving the change for my kid heading off to college. Everyone talks about how sad, tragic, and depressing things are once your child leaves home. I agree. Everything is different. There is no teenager coming home to tell you about their day. There are no family plans for sporting events and weekend trips. There isn't a pile of friends showing up with an hour notice for a Star Wars Movie Marathon sleepover and midnight pizza runs.

The hub of activity in my home is now a hush of quiet and nothingness. At first, it felt like everything was a reminder of what was missing. There was the picture of the family trip to Oregon. Here was the bottle cap art project we did two summers ago. The empty room, which is now perfectly neat. The bed where he slept pretty much every night for the last eighteen years, sometimes with the door open and sometimes with the door closed.

Love the change? I'm trying.

If I focus the "what I have lost" parts, it's hard. But if I can focus on the "what's to love" idea, it changes things. I can love having half the normal grocery bill. I can love having more time with my spouse. I can enjoy having a bit more space in my day. Now I can pursue things I am passionate about like writing, working, serving others, volunteering, creating. I have space in my day to be present, to be available, to pray without distraction.

I'm not all the way there yet in loving the change. I can say I'm making progress towards a better place. There is a lot to love. For this moment, I will seek to be content in what is and to find ways to embrace the new season.

I'm grateful God has given me all those years of memories, stories, and blessings. I'm grateful my son has set off on his new adventure in college and beyond. I pray every day that he, too, will love this change and find more of how God has called him.

My hope is we raised a son who can now go out into the world and pour into and encourage others. My hope is that all those years of equipping have given him a foundation of confidence in a God who wants him to live boldly. We raised him to leave us and that is exactly what he has done.

I can't say loving the change fills me with happiness, but I know it's what is right. I can love the change of knowing this is the natural next step. I can love that he is becoming the man God intends him to be.

Think
How can you find ways to love the season you are in?

Chapter 7
RESOURCES

Resources for Renewal and Nourishment.

"Create in me a pure heart, O God, and renew a steadfast spirit within me." Psalm 51:10

My Homeschool Planning Worksheet

Why do I homeschool?

Know your why and write it here.

_____

_____

_____

_____

_____

_____

_____

_____

My Homeschool
Planning Worksheet

What is my elevator speech about homeschooling?
Explain in 30 seconds or less.

_____

_____

_____

_____

_____

_____

_____

_____

_____

My Homeschool Planning Worksheet

What are my three biggest concerns with homeschooling and how will I address them?

_____
_____
_____
_____
_____
_____
_____
_____
_____
_____

My Homeschool Planning Worksheet

By the time your child embarks on future plans outside the home, what would you hope they experience?

_____

_____

_____

_____

_____

_____

_____

_____

_____

_____

GOALS FOR THE YEAR

For the Student: This is your place to dream about the year ahead. Make your goals measureable and specfic. Be sure to check back on your progress.

For the Student: What do you want this year to look like? Brainstorm your personal goals, hopes, dreams and wishes for the school year ahead.

For the Student: What would you love to learn about this year, either through a traditional or informal experience?

For the Student: How would you like to grow specifically in your faith journey this year?

For the Student: How would you like to grow from a health and wellness standpoint?

www.CaraMcLauchlanLife.com

DESIGNING YOUR DREAM HIGH SCHOOL WORKSHEET

Class Match Brainstorm - My student's greatest strengths and classes that match that are:

Challenge Match Brainstorm - Areas where my student is challenged and classes that match that are:

Student Love Brainstorm: Things my student would love to experience before graduation:

Parent Love Brainstorm: Things as a parent I would love my child to experience before graduation:

www.CaraMcLauchlanLife.com

Faith Journey Brainstomr

Ideas for Growing Your Faith this School Year

Use this space to brainstorm with your student how they would like to strengthen their faith walk this year. List ideas for books, camps, retreats, and personal goals you and your student would like to consider for the year ahead. Consider completing separately as parent and student, then share and compare ideas.

My Book Bucket List

A wishlist of books our family would like to read before finishing high school.

My Life Skills Bucket List

A wishlist of lifeskills our family would like our student to experience or prepare before finishing high school.

Most states typically require four English classes including expository, research-based, essay and creative writing. Use the space below to consider ideas for your course planning. Be sure to check your state's requirements.

English Class Ideas:

Homeschooling Planning Sheet

CLASS IDEAS

Most states typically require two-four Math classes, depending on your plans after high school. Consider Algebra 1/Algebra 2, Geometry and Pre-Calculus in your planning. Use the space below to consider ideas for your course planning. Be sure to check your state's requirements.

Math Class Ideas:

Homeschooling Planning Sheet

CLASS IDEAS

Most states typically require 2-4 Science courses including Physical Science, Biology, Chemistry or Physics. Be sure to incorporate labs as much as possible for hands-on learning. Use the space below to consider ideas for your course planning. Be sure to check your state's requirements.

Science/Lab Class Ideas:

Homeschooling
Planning Sheet

CLASS IDEAS

Most states typically require 2-4 History/Social Studies courses including US History and
World History courses. Use the space below to consider ideas for your course planning.
Be sure to check your state's requirements.

History/Social Studies Class Ideas:

Homeschooling Planning Sheet

ELECTIVES CLASS IDEAS

Most states typically require a Physical Education course, two-four years of Foreign Language and several electives of your personal choice. Use the space below to consider ideas for your course planning. Be sure to check your state's requirements.

Phys. Ed/Foreign Language and Elective Ideas:

Homeschooling Planning Sheet

TRAVEL & OTHER IDEAS

What else would you and your student like to consider as part of your high school years? Internships, work, sports, travel, intensives or field trips. Use the space below to capture additional experiences your student would love to consider.

Travel, Extracurricular and Other Ideas:

Homeschooling Planning Sheet

LEADERSHIP & SERVICE IDEAS

What leadership/volunteer or service-based opportunities would you and your student like to consider as part of your high school years? Use the space below to capture additional leadership experiences your student would love to consider.

Ideas for Leadership & Service Opportunities:

TRANSCRIPT LOG
Tracking Log of Key Information for Transcript

Use this space to capture important details to include in your high school transcript. This may include volunteer/service hours, awards, extracurriculars, or anything that you would like to note and save for future reference.

TRANSCRIPT LOG
Tracking Log of Key Information for Transcript

Use this space to capture important details to include in your
high school transcript. This may include volunteer/service
hours, awards, extracurriculars, or anything that you would like
to note and save for future reference.

www.CaraMcLauchlanLife.com

TRANSCRIPT LOG

Tracking Log of Key Information for Transcript

Use this space to capture important details to include in your
high school transcript. This may include volunteer/service
hours, awards, extracurriculars, or anything that you would like
to note and save for future reference.

www.CaraMcLauchlanLife.com

Summer Planning Ideas

Ideas for adventures, camps, travel, books or other fun things my student or our family would like to consider for the summer season.

Summer Brainstorm with My Student:

End Notes

Heartsongs

1. Davis, Eric. *Raising Men*. St. Martin's Press, 2016.
2. *Experiencing God*. Henry T. Blackaby, 1993. B&H Books.

Mix It Up

1. Macaulay, Susan Schaeffer. *For the Children's Sake: Foundations of Education for Home and School*. 1998. Blackstone Audiobooks.

Behold

1. Simons, Ruth Chou. *Beholding and Becoming: The Art of Everyday Worship*. 2019. Harvest House.

Refresh

1. Cowman, L.B. *Streams in the Desert, 366 Daily Devotional Readings*. 1999. Zondervan.

About Cara McLauchlan

Cara McLauchlan delights in encouraging families with her words and ideas. She has published numerous articles and contributed to several books to inspire God's best in others. For the last ten years, she has mentored and tutored hundreds of families through the traditional and classical homeschooling model.

To learn more, visit www.CaraMcLauchlanLife.com.

CPSIA information can be obtained
at www.ICGtesting.com
Printed in the USA
BVHW071217300121
599036BV00001B/4